HEALING THE
Brokenhearted

Dear Mother –

Please enjoy this
book.

Sondra

HEALING THE
Brokenhearted

Overcoming the Dangers of Spiritual Injuries

LUIS R. SCOTT, SR.

Ordering Information:

For orders and inquiries, please contact:
1-888-375-9818
www.toplinkpublishing.com
bookorder@toplinkpublishing.com

Printed in the United States of America

CONTENTS

Dedication vii

Introduction
    The Journey Begins ix
Chapter 1
    The Cries of a Broken Heart 1
Chapter 2
    The Foggy Field: Emotional Confusion 36
Chapter 3
    Blinds Spots: Instinctive Reactivity 59
Chapter 4
    Family Secrets: Hidden in Plain Sight 98
Chapter 5
    Transparency: Learning to Trust Again 129
Chapter 6
    Trusting: Learning to Love Again 148
Chapter 7
    Spiritual Health: Becoming Whole 163
Appendix A
    List of Spiritual Injuries 185

About the Author... 187

DEDICATION

I dedicate this book to every person who has suffered catastrophic spiritual injuries, and who has fallen into the cycle of shame that has led them to self-destructive behaviors and dysfunctions. To those whose hearts were broken by loved ones, and who have survived their brokenness, I pray they will learn to trust and love again. I also pray that God's grace and healing power of the Holy Spirit bring you peace of mind so that you can mend your broken heart.

INTRODUCTION
The Journey Begins

I attended the United States Army Chaplain Officer Basic Course Phase II from February to March 1991. One of the classes dealt with ethics and ethical decision-making. The chaplain instructor for the course began the class with the following statement (I am quoting from memory, but it is almost verbatim): "Every time I have a Hispanic chaplain in my class, I have an ethical dilemma. Since I know Hispanics are not qualified to be United States army chaplains, I know I should fail them. But since we invited them to be part of the chaplaincy, I have to give a passing grade to chaplains who are not qualified and should not be in the army."

I was one of two Hispanic chaplains in the class, and the instructor was obviously referring to us when he made his comments. I catapulted to my feet and forcefully challenge his racist remarks. He ignored me and continued his diatribe by adding that "Hispanics bring their wives to the United States and then prevent them from learning English, so they can beat them." My outrage boiled over, and my protests became louder and louder. Mercifully, the class came to a conclusion, and I left the classroom extremely angry and disappointed that another chaplain could hold such vitriolic views. Some of my classmates suggested that I should press charges for racism. Although I should have, I chose not to do it, probably out of fear to hurt my chances with the army. I just wanted to get out of there unscathed.

While I hardly ever mentioned the event, the insult was seared in my memory. Years later I realized the chaplain's statements had damaged me more than I had been aware of that day in the classroom. I can say with honesty I never held a grudge against the man, but

I also know those words became a spiritual injury that eventually turned into a blind spot. I will speak about blind spots in Chapter 4.

The instructor's words were a racially motivated indictment on my education, intelligence, and abilities. I knew I was qualified to be an army chaplain. I had the seminary degree to prove it. Not only that, I also had four years of experience as an infantry soldier. Prior military experience is not a requirement for the chaplaincy, but it does not hurt. I know now that I should not have allowed those words to play such a big role in my thinking and behavior, but they did. The instructor's words became an irreconcilable contradiction in my spirit. While I knew I was fully qualified to be an army chaplain, the instructor had associated my cultural background with my lack of qualifications. His words were false, and yet they left a permanent mark in me. Initially, I did not recognize the contradiction as a spiritual injury. I did not have a point of reference to adequately identify the damage the man's words had done.

It took me many years before I realized how damaging those words had truly been. The first indication that something was out of balance was when a good friend asked me why I always had to include my personal résumé in my conversations, especially when I met someone for the first time. Until she asked me the question, I had not realized how persistent this tendency had become. Her question forced me to take a closer look into this matter for the first time. With a little coaching and patience from my friend, I was able to see the compulsive nature of my reactions. After my friend made the observation, I began to make the conscious effort to control the subconscious and almost uncontrollable urge to defend my qualifications in every conversation. Whenever I knew I was meeting new people, I would tell myself to hold off on saying anything about myself. Initially, it was hard to keep my instinctive defensiveness in check. Eventually, the pressure subsided until my qualifications were no longer an issue. There is no doubt I had developed a blind spot. It had caused predictable and compulsive reactions every time I felt someone was questioning my qualifications. Sometimes I reacted defensively, even if no one had said anything. As a result of my reactivity, on many occasions, I wrongly anticipated people's negative attitudes when no such attitude was present.

During my struggle to understand why I was reacting in such a predictable way, I identified two behaviors directly connected to the spiritual injury. First, I was expressing an unconscious need to explain my educational and intellectual qualifications during casual conversations when the explanation was not necessary or requested. I was in a constant defensive posture regarding my competence. I became convinced that my defensiveness was directly connected to the spiritual injury dating back the incident at the chaplains' school. The ethics instructor's words created in me the false belief that everybody thought I was unqualified, solely based on my cultural heritage. My perception was wrong and so, was my reaction to it. The reality is that most people do not question, or care, about my competence. My qualifications could become an issue to people only if I show that I am over my head in my job. My perception of people's opinions had become an issue for me, and I had developed the need to provide unrequested explanations. In spite of the turmoil I was experiencing, the compulsion to defend my qualifications in almost every conversation remained hidden to me for years.

Thankfully, I did not lose any friends along the way. The spiritual injury did not impair my ability to conduct professional ministry overall, but after my friend pointed out my tendency, I accepted the possibility that I may have turned off some clients during counseling. However, there was one benefit that resulted from the injury. I became very sensitive and empathic (often too empathic) with people who were put down and abused by others. I still go out of my way to ensure that I treat people with the dignity God has blessed them with, regardless of the circumstances. Still, there is no doubt that the spiritual injury affected how I presented myself, especially around people I admired for their intellect and experience.

The second indicator was very similar to the first. I would become instinctively angry when someone talked down to me. I would also become angry when I witnessed someone else being talked down to. If I even suspected that other people had an attitude of superiority, I would react with noticeable dislike and, on occasions, with overt anger. Since I had never been an angry person, many times, I would be surprised and become upset by my reactions.

The most difficult aspect of dealing with the spiritual injury was accepting the unpleasant fact that I had allowed another person to exercise this kind of power over me. Most people would reject the possibility that another person can have such an impact on us because we believe we are the rulers of our destinies. A stranger should not be able to injure us like this. After my friend pointed out my reactive tendency to defend my qualifications, I had to make a decision: Either, I take a closer look at my behavior and make adjustments or reject my friend's observations and drive on without changing. I am thankful for my friend's coaching and patience. Her observation gave me the opportunity to take the necessary steps to recognize the injury for what it was and adjust my reactions to people. While I cannot erase the injury because the scar and the memories remain, I no longer feel compelled to give my résumé in casual conversation.

Purpose of this Book

This book has two main purposes. First, I want to share the principles I have discovered in working with people with crippling spiritual injuries and how we can provide hope in the midst of despair. Second, I want to bring awareness to the serious challenges spiritual injuries represent to the church and to the devastating consequences they have in people's lives. Since most people have experienced spiritual injuries to one degree or another, the church needs to work on finding solutions to the dysfunctions created by the more serious spiritual injuries. Jesus said that the church would have the power to heal the afflicted. Jesus "called his twelve disciples to him and gave them authority to drive out evil spirits and to heal every disease and sickness" (Matt. 10:1). While many have used a restrictive interpretation of this passage (that the command was exclusive to the disciples of that era or that this could be limited to physical illnesses), other passages indicate that Jesus's followers, in addition to the original disciples, were also given the same authority to heal sickness and diseases. For instance, James stated the following:

Is any one of you in trouble? He should pray. Is anyone happy? Let him sing songs of praise. Is any one of you sick? He should call the elders of the church to pray over him and anoint him with oil in the name of the Lord. And the prayer offered in faith will make the sick person well; the Lord will raise him up. If he has sinned, he will be forgiven. (Jam. 5:13-15)

James gave a specific process on how church leaders should pray for believers with different types of ailments. The apostle left the impression that the church's authority was inclusive. In addition to praying for the sick, God would even forgive people's sins if those were present. Therefore, Jesus's command to his disciples to heal the sick was more inclusive than some have allowed. The command extended beyond Jesus's historical moment and unto the church's mission to the world.

I do not think Jesus limited the church's healing ministry to ulcers and headaches. The text appears to make a distinction between diseases and sicknesses. The difference between these two words might appear, on the surface, to be about semantics, but I think Jesus had two distinct forms of maladies in mind. The Greek word for disease *voson* (νοσον) is related to undetermined types of maladies, such as mental illnesses and even demon possession.[1] Jesus, then, used a different word for sickness *malakia* (μαλακια). This word has the more specific meaning of "bodily weaknesses" such as leprosy, paralysis, or blindness.[2] The difference between these words lies in the undetermined aspect of the word *disease* versus the more definite meaning of physical ailments, as the word "*malakia*" implies.

The church can take a leading role in healing all types of illnesses, to include the paralyzing effect of spiritual injuries. I am convinced the church has not fully explored the treatment of self-destructive behaviors as a ministry. Perhaps this ministry remains untouched

---

[1] Joshua Dickey. The Complete Koine-English Reference Bible: New Testament, Septuagint and Strong's Concordance (Kindle Location 437675). Kindle Edition.)

[2] Ibid.

because it's hard work. Often deeply spiritually injured people live in an emotional rock bottom or they are just one step away from it. Most churches have not figured out how to effectively enter the spiritual-health world. It is less risky to give money to charities that deal with *those* people than to get directly involved with them. I believe every church should develop a ministry to combat spiritual brokenness, with the same intensity we approach the issues related to eternal life and discipleship. The idea is that that more Christian ministries should take the necessary steps to invest some of their resources in spiritual healing ministries. It's important to add that spiritual health ministries are long on hours and the require a great deal of patience. Additionally, we need to train the people involved in healing ministries to develop the staying power to see their own healing process through to its conclusion.

Finally, I want to bring awareness of the pervasive nature of spiritual brokenness in our society. In our research with more than 2,700 subjects over a period of three years, suffering from different types of addictive behaviors, I found that 100 percent of them suffered some form of a catastrophic spiritual injury (physical, sexual, or emotional abuse). I do not intend, nor pretend, to have the final answer on this subject. However, I want to start a discussion that could free people from the subconscious compulsion to engage in self-destructive behaviors. We can bring hope to people suffering from spiritual injuries and help them live more satisfying lives if we embark in the process of healing the many, and often unrecognized, spiritual injuries many of us have experienced.

Approach

While my basic presuppositions are biblically based, the concepts arose from my analysis of the 2,700 subjects that came to our treatment facility. I need to clarify that, in spite of the Christian foundation, this is not a book intended to evangelize or to seek converts. Nevertheless, I hope that in the process of learning about spiritual injuries, many people would come to the realization that intimacy with God is intrinsically tied to people's spiritual health. Any lasting friendships require a level of transparency, which is expressed in trust. However, people who have experienced catastrophic spiritual injuries have a hard time trusting other people because they have a broken intimacy mechanism. My desire is that more people will pursue spiritual health, so they can overcome the self-destructive behaviors that have caused so much misery and pain to so many people.

People's decision to seek spiritual health is crucial to conquer shame, guilt, and the self-destructive behaviors. These three issues will eventually rob people of their desire to live. Since each person has a unique story, we cannot use a one size fits all approach to spiritual health. Nevertheless, there are enough common denominators in the visible symptoms people exhibit that we can make generalized suggestions for a healing process.

The Christian principles I discuss in this book are designed to meet as many needs as possible, while recognizing that I may not be able to reach everyone. I also understand that people who are not spiritually inclined may not benefit from this book because my presuppositions are distinctively Christian. However, since human nature is fairly predictable, regardless of the person's faith, I hope that many non-Christians would consider the validity of the possible solutions presented here. Spiritual injuries have touched people from all walks of life, regardless of their beliefs system. This is the reason I invite you to continue this journey with us as we pursue spiritual health together. While some of you may not be followers of Christ, and the solutions we present here are based on the Christian ethic, I understand if you feel hesitant. However, I would encourage you to stay with this process to completion for the sake of your spiritual health. For, if you are trapped in any form of addictive behavior, this book is designed to get you to escape rock bottom. I recognize also that some Christians may not benefit from the approaches presented here. That said, my intent is to reach as many people as possible without distinction.

As you can imagine, each personal story is as unique as the individuals themselves. Upon closer examination, however, the underline problem for all spiritual injuries is basically the same—a spiritual impairment that prevents people from managing their lives without some form of addictive or self-destructive behavior. Many people have chosen to drink, use hard drugs, or be addicted to sex as the means to self-medicate their deep, but invisible, spiritual wounds. I have discovered that the great majority of people who have experienced a catastrophic spiritual injury do not know how their needs for self-medication are directly connected to their spiritual brokenness. Without being fully aware of the consequences of their decisions, the choice to self-medicate only results in multiplying the damage of the already present spiritual injuries. With each drink, illegal drug, or sexual escapade, the self-inflicted wounds become more pronounced and the pain less manageable. After years of indulging in the chosen dysfunction, the original spiritual injury becomes confused with the dysfunction. The self-destructive behaviors hide the pain for short periods of time, but they do not resolve the hidden and often severe brokenness. Every person who falls into the self-medication trap claims to have a valid external reason for the addiction, but all those addictions are the result of the spiritual injury. Regardless of the excuses people give, every person trapped by shame and guilt are profoundly unhappy with whom they have become. This book seeks to bring hope to the brokenhearted.

The Decision

People have asked the same question over and over. How could intelligent people, who know and understand the dangers of addictions and who realize they are losing control over their lives, are still unable to stop their inclination to destructive behaviors? I have concluded that people are not ignorant regarding the consequences of their addictions, and they do not become addicted because they are morally bankrupt. Like everybody else, people with destructive behaviors aspire to live normal lives. In spite of their best wishes, however, the spiritually injured person drifts into a disappointing and unfulfilled life. I have looked for answers for their plight. Their pain is, at times, overwhelming, and as a result they self-medicate. This is not a conscious decision. Self-medication is a craving for relief and a cry for help. What can be done, if anything, to bring a ray of hope to spiritually injured people in the midst of despair?

Initially, I did not have many answers, but I kept taking notes and trying to put together characteristics shared by people with identifiable self-destructive behaviors. After years of study, I realized that people with broken spirits shared at least two characteristics: first, they do not realize their behaviors have become predictable and impulsive, and, second, they do not know how to escape rock bottom without help. As a general rule, self-destructive behaviors are a superficial solution for a deeper spiritual brokenness.

Self-destructive behaviors have at least two other negative consequences. First, the spiritual injuries have impaired and crippled the addicted persons' ability to be at peace with themselves, with others, or with God. The are not at peace with themselves because of a deep restlessness in which it is too scary for them to be alone. This fear also has a negative impact on people's ability to relate with others because of the false belief that no one cares about them or is interested in their well-being. Spiritual injuries take many names and forms, but the end results are the same—a deeply felt spiritual emptiness and restlessness caused by a broken ability to engage in healthy emotional relationships with other people. Some people were physically abused. Others were sexually abused. Others were abandoned. Still others suffered through their parents' divorce and blamed themselves for their parents' failure. These types of injuries have the common denominator of producing a shame-based existence. Spiritually injured people are very aware that their addictive behaviors are killing them. However, most of them are oblivious that their self-destructive behaviors are directly tied to their spiritual brokenness. They are also indicators that the deeply felt spiritual brokenness is taking them to rock bottom. It's at this point that people can give up on life or choose to fight to overcome their paralyzing plight.

I need to clarify one thing. I am not making excuses for people with self-destructive behaviors or addictions. An argument can be made that people consciously choose to engage in addictive behaviors. However, an argument can also be made that the *choices* to engage in self-destructive behaviors are more influenced by the uncontrollable need to reduce their spiritual pain than from the desire to be cool or to fit in. They do need to fit in, to be sure, and in many occasions the need to fit in is the result of the spiritual injury. People need to feel

normal in spite of their belief that they don't fit in. Like the rest of us, they need to be accepted as contributing members of their social environment.

Second, spiritual injuries are killing the people suffering them but most of the time they do not know why they are dying, even though the answer resides within. Many have attempted suicide. Others have lost their families or their jobs. Their suffering is as real as it gets. Once injured people get hooked to the activity that brings temporary relief, they become dually enslaved, first to the pain caused by the injury and then to the addictive behavior that follows it. These people are now in a desperate race to control or to reduce the unrecognizable pain. As a result, they have become dependent on the self-destructive behaviors that will eventually kill them. Brokenhearted individuals cannot recognize the pain because they cannot pinpoint its origin. While they know about the spiritual injury, they can't connect it to the present dysfunction. In this sense, the self-medicating compulsion has substituted their desire to live pain free with the controlling desire for temporary relief. Once injured individuals enter this vicious cycle additional physical problems begin to emerge.

In most instances, brokenhearted individuals need independent intervention to overcome the pains that are killing them. The solution starts with stopping or slowing down the physical damage to which the individuals subject themselves as a result of their addiction. Not only do individuals suffer from what appears to be an unstoppable pain, but they also suffer from a crippling shame and that damage their social skills. The consequences of the addiction are very real and physically noticeable.

In order to identify spiritual injuries, we must first come to terms with the reality of the spiritual pain that drives the individuals to self-destructive behaviors. This is a crucial aspect of the healing process. The pain manifests itself in predictable symptoms that point back to the original spiritual injury. The first symptom I will discuss is the foggy field. This symptom is an indicator that a traumatic event took place in the person's life. Failure to address the spiritual pain could easily turn the individuals back to their old dysfunctional behaviors.

CHAPTER 1

The Cries of a Broken Heart

The call came in around 10:45 a.m. I arrived at the young soldier's house to find the horror of a twenty-six years old wife and mother of two children dead. She had taken her gun and shot herself on the chest. A neighbor had called the military police because she had heard what sounded to her like a gunshot and had become concerned. By the time the military police and the ambulance arrived at the house, it was too late. She was gone. In a decision made on a split second, she left her husband and two small children behind. They would now have to grow up without their mother. This young woman did not want to die. How do we know this? She was driven to this decision by persistent sexual harassment in her work place. She left a nine pages long letter detailing the harassment, the steps she took to address the issue with her superiors and the answers she received from them. The tipping point came when her supervisor decided to take administrative action against her for slandering the harassers. Her commanding officer, who happened to be a woman, wanted to reduce her in rank for making her complaints known.

Of all the injustices I have seen in my life, this one was the most blatant and vicious. The supervisors believed the stories of the men who had been harassing this young soldier. The two men would corner her on the hallways and fondled her against her will. The assaults lasted for more than a year, until she could not manage it any more. The young woman had suffered two spiritual injuries. She was injured when two of her fellow soldiers had taken it upon themselves to take advantage of her. The harassers did not care that she was a fellow soldier or that she was married to another soldier. The sexual harassment became an irreconcilable contradiction that

caused her enormous spiritual pain. The second injury came when her supervisors blamed her and decided to punish her for defending herself. This was her tipping point. She arranged her finances to make sure the bills were paid on time. Finally, she wrote letters to her husband and children. After all her businesses were in order, in a moment of desperation, her young and promising life was over.

This young woman had suffered a catastrophic spiritual injury caused by the trauma of being subjected to persistent sexual harassment. She suffered alone to avoid a possible violent confrontation if she told her husband. When all her options had vanished, she made the worst decision possible. She felt trapped and hopeless. Every member of her chain of command had failed her. After the damaged had been done, they were fired, and the army settled a multi-million dollars lawsuit for wrongful death. All of it could have been avoided if someone, anyone, would have done their jobs and investigated the harassment.

Clearly, not all spiritual traumas end with this type of tragedy, but all spiritual injuries leave trails of suffering on their paths. For the rest of this book we will define the spiritual injuries concept, the consequences of those spiritual traumas, and conclude with a process that provides hope for the brokenhearted.

A Definition of Spiritual Injury

A spiritual injury is the result of a traumatic event that produces *an irreconcilable contradiction between what people instinctively believe to be true, about themselves and the world around them, and what is actually true.* The traumatic event could be a fall, a vehicle accident, physical or sexual abuse, a rape, sexual harassment, or just words that create and irreconcilable contradiction. The key to understanding spiritual injuries is not the trauma itself. While the trauma plays a significant role in producing the contradiction, we know many people who have suffered similar traumas without developing into spiritual injuries. In order for a spiritual injury to develop, the trauma must produce an irreconcilable contradiction in the person. Without the irreconcilable contradiction, from the

perspective of this book, there will not be a lasting spiritual injury that can alter the person's character.

Let me add that a spiritual injury is a logical or an emotional contradiction between an expected norm and the actual results produced by the trauma. That is, when people's expectations of how the world *should* function do not match their experienced reality, as a result of a traumatic event, a spiritual injury could occur. For example: most people believe that one of the expectations of marriage is to stay together until death do them part. If one of the partners chooses to divorce or to leave, the other partner could experience an irreconcilable contradiction between what they believe to be true (that they should stay together until death do them part) and what has actually happened (they divorced before their deaths). If they fail to reconcile their belief that they should stay together with the reality that one of the spouses left before death, this contradiction could become a spiritual injury. The initial indicator that people who experience divorce may have suffered a spiritual injury is a sudden emotional confusion that prevents them from making logical decisions. This spiritual and emotional state of confusion is what I call the foggy field. Before I discuss the foggy field later in the book, let me share a few foundational concepts that can guide our discussion.

Irreconcilable Contradictions

An irreconcilable contradiction emerges when one visible and undeniable physical experience distorts a clearly defined and deeply held belief. Most of us cannot live with emotional contradictions. We must find a solution. Any irreconcilable contradiction lodged in our consciousness will create emotional restlessness. The sharper the contradiction, the greater the anxiety it produces. People have several prominent responses to irreconcilable contradictions. Some people give up on their efforts to make sense of the trauma and the subsequent feelings of restlessness by burying the event that caused it. This means that if a child believes his father is a decent man, but the father is a drunk, the child will hold on to his belief and, either,

make excuses for his father's drunkenness, or go into complete denial about his father's failures.

Another response some people may have is to re-live the catastrophic event, preventing them from recognizing the contradiction. This response can send them into a journey to self-destructive behaviors and addictions. When people are constantly reliving their traumas, they will have a hard time overcoming their pain. It is of critical importance for the person to develop a sense of hope about the future in order to understand their trauma and pain from a more hopeful possibility. The same child, who lived with an alcoholic father, could end up following in his father's footsteps because if he could be a good man as an alcoholic so can he. In this case, the son imitates the symptom of the father's spiritual injury. In all likelihood, the father became an alcoholic to self-medicate his own spiritual pain, but the son does not know what caused the father's irreconcilable contradiction. Thus, the son becomes an alcoholic to overcome the pain caused by the contradiction that his father was unreliable, abusive, and sick, but these are secondary effects of the father's initial trauma. This is the reason that the son's addiction is not directly related to his father's spiritual injury. It's the symptom of it. His heart is broken for a different reason, but the consequences are almost identical, a life consumed by addictive behaviors.

There is also the possibility of a rejection. The son could have a reaction of disgust against his father for his failure to be the role model the son needed and desired. It is not uncommon for the grown children of alcoholic families to move as far away from their families as soon as they can to avoid the father's drunkenness. All they want is to escape the family secrets and dysfunctions. These adult children could also become physically violent against their parents for creating a hostile environment in the home. They will blame the father for all the family dysfunctions, and the mother for enabling the father's addictions. As a result of these blame games, they look with some anticipation to the day the father is no longer tormenting the family, or when the mother is finally able to stand up to their father.

Causes of Spiritual Injuries

Simply put, spiritual injuries are the result of physically or emotionally traumatic events that produce an irreconcilable contradiction in people's consciousness. These events distort people's understanding of reality. For instance, rapes produce a fear in women that can prevent them from establishing intimate and healthy relationships with men, while physical abuse can turn happy children into somber and violent adults. These types of physical injuries will leave permanent emotional wounds in people's hearts. Betrayals and abandonments by a spouse or parents are examples of non-physical events (spiritual if you will) that could result in a broken heart. In some cases, children, and even adults, could feel a deep sense of abandonment when a parent suffers an untimely death or an unexpected separation and divorce. The young woman who committed suicide, in the earlier story, was betrayed by her immediate supervisors and even the commanding officers in her army unit. She was deeply injured by the contradiction that the people who should have protected her, had in fact betrayed her.

People have the innate desire for inner peace in their relationships– whether these are between nations, tribes, marriages, or families. When parents or spouses die, individuals may feel as if the loved one abandoned them without cause. Some people even blame themselves for the passing of the loved one. But, obviously, no one dies intentionally to abandon their families and, especially, their children. Even people who commit suicide do not intend to abandon their families. These people have reached an unbearable brokenness that abandoning life is not only an option, but the only solution to their predicament. Even in these instances, their intention is not to abandon their loved ones. This is especially true when people who commit suicide leave notes seeking forgiveness or expressing regret. Some people who choose suicide go as far as to arrange the family finances to make sure their families are *taken care* off after they are gone.

Above all, most people desire to have an intimate relationship with God. But if they blame God for their suffering, then, in their minds, turning to him for protection is not a viable option. The apostle

Paul mentioned that we were "hostile in our minds" against God (Col. 1:21). This hostility comes from spiritual injuries, disappointments, and blaming God for our suffering and failures. In this scenario, inner peace is a vanishing dream until people accept that their needs for friendship with God is intrinsic to who they are and begin to establish a personal relationship with him. It is only then that people can regain their capacity to establish a transparent intimacy with God and others. The journey to spiritual health, then, is the process to rebuild the intimacy mechanism so that people can love again. A healthy intimacy mechanism allows people to trust again, and with trust comes transparency, which is the fundamental element for healthy intimacy with God and people. That was Moses's message regarding the shame Adam and Eve felt in the Garden that drove them to hide from God after becoming aware of good and evil. If we understand Moses correctly, Adam and Eve lost their capacity to be spiritually transparent with God.

The Illusiveness of Spiritual Pain

As it probably has become clear to the reader, the term spiritual injury is a metaphor intended to make a parallel comparison with physical injuries. Physical injuries produce intense pain from broken bones or bleeding resulting from lacerations of the skin. Physical pain has at least one benefit. It focuses people's attention, like a laser beam, to the location on the body in which the injury occurred. Similarly, spiritual injuries produce an intense emotional brokenness in the person's soul. The difference between the two types of injuries is that while the spiritual pain is as real as the physical one, people cannot pinpoint the *location* of their spiritual pain. The pain is real, but the remedy is not readily apparent. A feeling of restlessness in the soul, or a lack of emotional peace, is the clearest indicator that a spiritual injury has occurred. Once the restlessness has been identified, the long journey to identifying the blind spot (or the lie) created by the spiritual injury can begin.

This process is not simple nor painless. In many occasions, the discovery of the spiritual injury can revive the emotional trauma of

the original injury. This process always presents a risk in which the presuppositions that have allowed the person to hide the original contradiction could come down like a house of cards. As a result of this process, the superficial *truths* they had believed for most of their lives must give way to a new reality based on truth. When Jesus said, "Come to me, all you who are weary and burdened, and I will give you rest" (Matt. 11:28), he probably had this process in mind. Injured people need an existential truth beyond themselves in order to replace the lie created by the irreconcilable contradiction. Only the truth can provide them safety and lasting peace. Most of us would recognize that a broken heart has physical and emotional symptoms. Some of the physical symptoms include things like headaches and indigestion. And the emotional symptoms could include things such as depressive moods, isolation, panic attacks, and other forms of anxiety.

Spiritual injuries also restrict people's ability to overcome adversity. Since the primary impulse is to avoid anything that may remind them of the event that caused their pain, they would flee from any situation that can revive their painful memories. Most of these people become instinctively reactive to any situation that may remind them of the original trauma. Others may project their dysfunctions outwardly. And others may simply avoid these types of situations altogether. Regardless of the choice they make, their lack of coping skills will hinder conflict resolution or the possibility of overcoming the adversity they face. We can agree that this kind of brokenness is not easily repaired. The biggest challenge people may face in the process to heal their broken hearts is found in the difficulty of connecting the spiritual pain they have always felt to the event that caused it. Most people remember the trauma, and they know very well how they feel about it. One of the problems is that most people do not know how the original trauma altered their characters to make them reactive to events that remind them of the event that caused their pain. Additionally, some people become susceptible to similar temptations, and in the worst cases, some become prone to addictive, compulsive or self-destructive behaviors.

Whenever people do not have inner peace, in all likelihood, they have experienced some form of spiritual injury. Their restlessness is generally manifested as an absence of spiritual and emotional

peace with God, self, and others. In most cases, this restlessness is a good indicator that a catastrophic spiritual injury has occurred, but it remains unidentified or improperly addressed. If we are going to understand our spiritual sensitivity to abuse and neglect, we need to consider how God created us in his image.

The Power of Words

The Bible says that "death and life are in the power of the tongue" (Prov. 18:21). Clearly, Solomon was not saying this physical muscle had such power. If you ask any doctor, they would say that the heart, the kidneys, or the lungs are more determinative for life and death than the tongue. Of course, I believe Solomon was referring to the power of words. Many people have been injured by words as deeply as they have been by external traumatic events. Similarly, many people have overcome incredible odds by maintaining a positive attitude and declaring their desire to survive. Let me share an example regarding the power of words.

Sophie and Anthony had been married for four years. He was an architect, and she was a nurse. They appeared to be the perfect couple. They were young and attractive, but according to her, they were going to get a divorce. The obvious question was, why? Sophie stated that she had set up a key holder on the kitchen wall, but Anthony never hung his keys there. She took his carelessness as a sign of disrespect. When Sophie stated the reason for her desire to divorce, I was not sure if I should have exploded in laughter or if I should take her seriously. Since she looked so distraught, I decided not to laugh.

After several sessions, I began to suspected Sophie had demonstrated some obsessive-compulsive tendencies. Her dress was always perfect. She never had one hair out of place. I am sure her house had to be in perfect order, to include the key holder. Sophie had been projecting her obsessive compulsion anxiety (OCD) onto her husband. When she set up the key holder, she wanted to control her husband's behavior and Anthony became a hostage to a physical item that had nothing to do with their relationship and emotional

intimacy. I decided to test my theory to make sure I had read her responses correctly.

The next time Sophie and Anthony came for a visit I set my coffee table with about twenty magazines. I put them in total disorder and placed my coffee table close enough to the couch to observe what Sophie would do. Sure enough, as soon as she sat down, she began to organize the magazines. I observed her doing her handy work until she had made three rows of eight magazines each organized in alphabetical order. After she was done, I asked her why did she arranged my magazines? She said, without missing a beat, because they look better that way. At this point, I told her that I liked the magazines the way I had them, and since they were my magazines, she should not have rearranged them without my permission. She became very defensive and began to apologize. Immediately, I calmed her down and showed her how her compulsive behavior was having a negative influence in her attitude toward her husband in relationship to the key holder.

After I had driven the point home, I decided to take a huge risk. I asked Sophie how old was she when she was told that she would always be a failure? Upon hearing my question, Sophie became very quiet and started sobbing. I waited for about ten minutes until she composed herself. Finally, she looked up and said: "I was seven years old when my mother told me for the first time that I would always be a dumb blonde and that I would never amount to anything." Of course, I don't know why a mother would use those words against her own daughter, but those words marked Sophie for the rest of her life. From that time on, her main goal was to prove that her mother was wrong about her, and as a result she decided that she would become perfect at everything. After graduating from high school, Sophie joined the army and was a successful practical nurse. She had married an architect and her life appeared to be soaring. But her mother's words still resonated with her and she was now sabotaging her marriage. Down deep in her soul, she wanted to be happy, but she also believed she did not *deserve* happiness because she was too dumb for that. That conversation was a breakthrough and our sessions had a happy ending. Sophie did not divorce Anthony.

Sophie had believed a lie that, if left unchecked, it could have destroyed her happy marriage to a good man. Sophie's mother had told her she was just a dumb blond so many times, that the lie had become her truth. Here she was, successful in her own right, married to a very successful man, beautiful and still believing she could never amount to anything. Her idealized image of self was in shambles because she believed the lie that her blonde hair determined her intellectual capacity. She believed this lie even though her reality was that she had become very successful in her own right. Sophie had the value of the images reversed. While most people's idealized images of self are exaggerated hero perceptions, Sophie's view of herself was inferior to her real image.

Jesus stated that the truth sets people free (Jn. 8:32). When Sophie accepted that she had believed a lie, she was able to replace it with the truth of her own successful personal and professional life. She also needed to accept the truth that her previously held convictions were lies. I want to give the reader a couple of suggestions to identify the lies in their lives. It is clear that before people can accept the truth that sets them free, they have to come to terms with the lie that have enslaved them.

God's Word takes center stage in the process of replacing the lies with the truth. The Bible provides us with a perspective that is greater than our present circumstances. For example, if a young child was told that he is worthless, the Bible corrects this lie with God's declaration that we are created in His image (Gen. 1:26; 9:6). Since we are created in God's image, then, it is not possible we can be worthless to Him. And if we are valuable to God, then, we are valuable to ourselves and to others also.

As we came to the end of our sessions, I asked Sophie what was her lie? She articulated the lie thus: "My blond hair determines my intelligence." Once she was able to articulate her lie, I asked her what was the truth? She stated, "My blond hair has nothing to do with my intelligence." Then, I asked her one final question: what needs to happen next? She said she had to continue believing that her hair had nothing to do with her intelligence.

Sometimes God gives us the privilege to witness the end result of a miracle. Three years later a couple asked me to conduct their

wedding ceremony. I accepted their request and on the day of the wedding, as I waited for the guests, I saw Sophie and Anthony with two kids in tow coming for the wedding. She had a new hairdo and had dyed her hair brown. As soon as she saw me, she came directly to me and gave me a hug. The only thing she said was: "I am no longer a dumb blond." Her words were one of the greatest testimonies God had given me the privilege to see firsthand. We both laughed, and those were the only words we exchanged. That was the last time I saw Sophie, but she let me know the truth had finally won. Words are very powerful. Words can enslave people, or they can set them free. In Sophie's case, her mother's words enslaved her for most of her life, and her discovery of the truth set her free.

"Sticks and Stones…"

Plenty of people have used the familiar phrase that "sticks and stones may break my bones, but words will never hurt me" to indicate that words do not easily offend them. While I had never used this phrase before, I am a living witness to the fact that words can be as hurtful, or more, than some physical injuries. The phrase is a blatant cultural lie, and it is a likely indication that the person using the phrase has been the recipient of a verbal spiritual injury. After spending over thirty-eight years working with brokenhearted people, I have arrived at four different, but interconnected, conclusions.

First, every person has experienced, to one degree or another, multiple spiritual injuries. Many people have suffered some form of rejection. Many of us come from broken homes. Others have been physically and sexually abused. Still others have experienced various degrees of abandonment. These experiences are stored in our consciousness and shape our characters and perceptions of the world around us. Every spiritual injury leaves a mark, but not everyone reacts to them with self-destructive behaviors. Minor spiritual injuries could be compared to the small scratches suffered while playing ball in the park. Like physical superficial scratches, these types of spiritual injuries do not have a significant or lasting effect on how people behave or perceive the world. Minor spiritual injuries can

still shape people's characters, and they could be an indication that a person is spiritually *accident-prone*. These spiritual scratches are incidental and non-determinative in character formation. However, when people experience catastrophic spiritual injuries, the damage could be severe, and the dysfunction could become spiritually and emotionally crippling.

Second, undiscovered catastrophic spiritual injuries almost always lead to dysfunctional relationships with people and God. People who have suffered catastrophic spiritual injuries have the tendency to drift into an accelerated dying process. They engage in destructive habits such as smoking, excessive drinking, drug abuse, and predatory sexual behavior that destroy their self-esteem and their overall feeling of being a good or worthy person. Most people are not aware of the significant role catastrophic spiritual injuries have played in their character formation. As a result, people have the tendency to react to the world as if their dysfunctional perceptions defined the world, rather than to view the world from the perspective of a healthy heart.

Third, one of the most dangerous aspects of catastrophic spiritual injuries is the development of blind spots. The more damaging the injury, the larger the blind spot. These blind spots produce predictable reactions to events and circumstances. They render the person unable to anticipate or control their reactions to those circumstances. Have you ever heard a person say, "People are always pushing my hot buttons"? The phrase indicates the instinctive and predictable reactions people have when spiritually sensitive areas are touched. People are not always aware how blind spots develop or how they impair their capacity to defend themselves against relational temptations or become susceptible to addictive behaviors. One thing is certain, blind spots are *always* the result of a catastrophic spiritual injury.

Third, catastrophic spiritual injuries damage, what I call, the intimacy mechanism. A broken intimacy mechanism leaves people with negative perceptions of self that hinder their ability to have honest friendships with other people. When I ask people about the source of their destructive behaviors, certain phrases constantly appear. "I am the black sheep of the family." "Nothing good ever happens to me."

"Everybody hates me." "I am not lovable." These negative self-talk phrases are indicators that the person's intimacy mechanism has been damaged. I believe self-destructive behaviors and negative self-talk run counter to a person's need for self-preservation. While many people get entangled in self-destructive behaviors, I don't believe they want to die. Even though people want to live, many of them appear to be in a rush to an early grave. Most people want to live free to pursue happiness. Down deep in their souls, these people do not want to live with the thought that they are God's worst project. Or worse, that they are an after-thought God uses to make others look good at their expense. When it appears that these people are rushing to their deaths, something must be spiritually out of place. How do people become so negative about themselves, or about living? I believe we are born with a positive desire toward life. If we talk with five years old children, we will not hear them complaining about life. The problem is, that once people experience disappointments their characters begin to change. If, in addition to their run of the mill disappointments, they also suffer catastrophic spiritual injuries, they will drift into a more negative perception of themselves. Regardless of how people describe their journeys to compulsive and damaging behaviors, a close look at their histories will reveal the common denominator of blind spots caused by spiritual injuries that have not fully healed.

Fourth, most people with self-destructive behaviors want to be freed from the slavery and misery their spiritual injuries have produced. We seldom make the connection that exists between the spiritual injuries and the resulting behavior and character formation that follows. The issue is not that people do not have a clear memory of the events that resulted in their spiritual injuries. This means that these individuals are not always aware of the resulting damage the spiritual injuries left in their intimacy mechanism. Their spiritual brokenness has remained hidden deep within their souls for years. Therefore, most people are not able to identify possible cures for the persistent inner pain the trauma produced in them. Since we are talking about a pain that resides within a people's souls, the pain is untraceable. As a result, their pain often drives many of them to self-medicate or to other compulsive behaviors. Such obsessive behaviors

vary based in the individual and can include: dependency on addictive substances, becoming workaholics, compulsive cleanliness, inability to sustain healthy relationships, becoming a hypochondriac, or it can manifest in sexually promiscuity. Regardless of the exhibited dysfunction, the spiritual pain becomes so persistent that it focuses all the person's energies in getting rid of the uncontrollable pain by any means necessary.

Spiritual Injuries Caused by External Events

I have identified two primary forms of spiritual injuries: (1) those caused by external events and (2) those that are self-inflicted. External events are, by far, the primary cause for catastrophic spiritual injuries. For our purposes I define external events as any action, statement, or circumstance over which people have little or no control. Other people, or unforeseen circumstances are the causes of these events. On many occasions these events could even be accidents that caught us by total surprise.

For example, Joni Eareckson Tada was paralyzed at the age of seventeen from a diving accident as she was training for a diving competition. Her response to her trauma has been nothing short of exemplary. She became a powerful Christian witness of God's grace. She has blessed millions of people of words of encouragement, and her ministry has also blessed thousands of people who have suffered similar injuries by donating wheelchairs and other life sustaining equipment. Billy Graham had this to say about this extraordinary woman: "Joni is an extraordinary person, yet her real strength and creativity come from a vital relationship with Jesus Christ."[3] Eareckson-Tada used her injury as an opportunity to manifest God's grace, but she is the exception. Most people simply crawl into a fetal position and wither away.

Joni's faith that propelled her to become a national spiritual leader. She has been a powerful example because she did not let the physical

---

[3] Joni Eareckson Tada. Joni: An Unforgettable Story (Kindle Location 50). Zondervan. Kindle Edition.

injury to become a crippling spiritual one. It could have happened very easily, but she fought back until she became a spokesperson to people suffering from all kinds of paralysis.

Many people fall victim of events and situations, not of their own making, that produce serious spiritual damage. These spiritual injuries caused by external events have two primary manifestations: (1) relational spiritual injuries that damage the intimacy mechanism have a negative effect on people's ability to relate with others, and (2) personality dysfunctions spiritual injuries that damage people's perception of self. Allow me to share a few statements about each.

Relational Spiritual Injuries

As a general rule, these spiritual injuries are the result of sexual abuse, in all its forms, from child abuse to rape. Like all spiritual injuries, they create irreconcilable contradictions that distorts people's understanding of intimate relationships. The person who has been sexually abused will have the tendency to view all types of relationships from a sexual perspective. These people can have friends, but they will see their friends as potential sexual partners, even if the sexual encounter never materializes. In some instances, people who have been sexually abused, as children or even as adults, could develop an instinctive repulsion to sexual intimacy and relationships in general. They need and want as much emotional intimacy as anyone else, but they do not know how to have healthy friendships or healthy intimacy with a lifetime partner. Even those who are repulsed by sex would have a strong tendency to engage in multiple relationships because the spiritual intimacy they desire never comes.

For instance, when children are sexually abused, their relational compass is distorted. They could develop the tendency to view all affinity to other people through a sexual prism. In sexual abuse cases, the victim could become overly promiscuous, sexually needy, hostile to sexual advances, and in many cases, these victims could develop sexual identity confusion or sexual dysphoria. Relational spiritual injuries cause damage to the intimacy mechanism preventing

people from developing healthy, loving, and emotionally intimate relationships with God and others. Even though the individuals *participated* in the sexually abusive event, they did so without their consent. In these cases, the events happened to them. These relational injuries, especially when the perpetrators are family members or close family friends, are particularly damaging because the people they trusted to protect their privacy, violated it. Make no mistake about it, these are violent events that will cause permanent damage to the intimacy mechanism and distort people's abilities to relate with others.

In each one of these examples, the injured individuals are victims of events and decisions that are beyond their control. A girl who is sexually abused by her stepfather cannot reconcile her belief that her protector has become her perpetrator. The boy abandoned by his parents cannot reconcile the belief that he should grow up in an emotionally safe and intimate relationships with his parents, but his reality is that his parents left him. The raped woman cannot reconcile her beliefs that no one has the right to violate her dignity, with the reality that someone forced her into a sexual act, without her consent that caused both physical and spiritual damage.

Personality Dysfunctions

These types of injuries are different than the relational injuries in that they do not necessarily have a negative effect of people's abilities to be emotionally and sexually intimate with other people. Their sexuality is not an issue. These types of injuries have a negative effect on people's perception of their self-worth. For instance, if a child does not make the baseball team or the cheerleaders team in elementary school, this rejection could develop into a pattern of negative self-fulfilling prophecies. If a young man is told that he is not smart enough to ever go to college, this could set him up for failure in his educational aspirations. The injury can rob him of his dreams.

People suffering from personality dysfunctions could become obsessive compulsive to prove they are as worthy as anyone else. Some of them become workaholics for the same reason. But the

majority of them simply surrender and accept that failure is God's plan for their lives. Fate had determined their outcome and there is nothing they can do about it. They move from one job to another unable to finish anything and always reflecting of their unworthiness as the reason for their unhappiness and failures. If they could regain a semblance of balance of their perception of self, their lives could turn around and they could finally find satisfaction with who they are, as God created them. This could be a long process, but one worthy to pursue.

Self-Inflicted Injuries

The second form of spiritual injuries is the self-inflicted. Generally speaking, self-inflicted spiritual injuries have little external influence. This type of injury is primarily the result of people making poor choices and decisions. Individuals who suffer self-inflicted spiritual injuries are mostly responsible for creating their own contradictions with their actions. As a result of that, their injuries become self-reflective. Since the injury comes from a bad decision, the person cannot escape the guilt and shame the injury produces because the individuals, themselves, are their own culprits. Self-inflicted injuries are as devastating as the externally caused injuries because the irreconcilable contradiction is internal, as appose to being external. I can cite two reasons for this.

First, people can always blame others or external circumstances for an external injury. Not so with a self-inflicted injury. With the self-inflicted injury, the blame falls on them for they are responsible for their own contradiction. It is more difficult to reconcile with the fact that we are responsible for creating our own spiritual contradiction and that our suffering is a direct result of our own actions.

Second, with self-inflicted injuries we cannot escape our victimizer—ourselves. This is one of the reasons victimizers work so hard at blaming their victims. When victims assume responsibility for their suffering, they become trapped in a vicious cycle of shame, and the victimizer can hide his shame on his victim's shame. But when we are responsible for our own injuries, there is no place to

hide. Some examples of self-inflicted injuries are: a divorce as the result of an affair, failure to finish a project that resulted in losing a job, robbing a convenience store and ending up in jail, indulging in recreational drugs and sex, and being abusive to others, perhaps even to family members. These self-inflicted injuries could have been influenced by external factors, but the individuals are still responsible for the consequences of their actions. If the individual ends up in jail, it does not matter what other factors influenced his decision, he is still the one incarcerated.

People who engage in extra marital affairs, for example, are personally injured by the affair, and later they are injured by the reconciliation process, or divorce. The innocent party receives an external injury as a result of the spouse's affair that is reinforced during the reconciliation process. Additionally, the innocent party can receive another injury if the couple decide to divorce. Spiritual injuries never happen in a relational vacuum. This means that spiritual and emotional traumas almost always take place within the individuals social context. This means that, whether we are dealing with an external or self-inflicted injury, other people will witness or experience the effect of our dysfunctions. Relational and dysfunctional injuries damage the intimacy mechanism, but the external manifestation of the dysfunction varies from person to person. This is the reason all catastrophic spiritual injuries can have such a devastating impact on people's ability to relate with others.

Let me make one more observation regarding the two types of spiritual injuries. Regardless of the source, many self-inflicted spiritual injuries can be traced to dysfunctions that have been passed from one generation to another by the family of origin. The abusive father could have been abused as a child. The rapist has a distorted view of sex and interpersonal relationships between men and women as a result of his own victimization or by watching family members victimize others, etc. This is not to say that we should blame all the ills that affect our society on our parents. But we cannot ignore how much influence our heritage has had on our present behavior. We can be proactive in the process of identifying our brokenness and look to God for guidance to find peace for our restless souls. Since we are spiritual and social creatures, our spiritual health begins and ends

with God and finds its most significant expression in our fellowship with our neighbor.

I believe that we can restore people to spiritual health, regardless of the severity of the spiritual trauma. However, I also recognize that there are some extreme cases in which the injured person might have reached a point of no return. This can happen when individuals fall into deep depression or when their addiction has destroyed their capacity to think rationally or their desire to live. The main reason for the despair is not that people cannot heal. The problem is that by the time we reach them, they are too far gone for any effective intervention to take place. That said, I am still convinced that, as long as people still have the desire to live, they can overcome the dysfunctional consequences of their broken hearts through a process of reconciliation, forgiveness, and restoration. This requires a process of self-discovery in which people can find their purpose for which God created them. This journey cannot be undertaken in isolation. I believe a Christian community of faith is the best place in which God's grace and love can be received and shared by those who are seeking restoration and spiritual health.

In addition to the above discussed subjects, spiritual injuries can be grouped into two main categories: (1) superficial, and (2) catastrophic. This book will focus on the second category but let me define each one to establish their differences.

Superficial Spiritual Injuries

Superficial spiritual injuries are the result of minor incidents that produce emotional and spiritual discomfort but are not serious enough to alter people's ability to relate with God and others. These types of injuries may turn into pet peeves, but they do not prevent people from conducting their lives in a normal or routine manner. Superficial injuries are not the result of a catastrophic event. Rather, they are the result of minor disagreements, confrontations, or physically embarrassing event, like slipping on an icy sidewalk. These events could be infuriating, but since they do not damage the intimacy mechanism people won't suffer permanent damage, even if they

develop mistrust for certain situations or become more cautious about dealing with people. Let me make a few observations regarding pet peeves before defining catastrophic spiritual injuries.

Pet Peeves

Pet peeves (or pet hate) are the most common manifestation of superficial spiritual injuries. A Pet Peeve is a minor annoyance that can instill great frustration in individuals. Some people could become quite agitated about their pet peeves. For example: Let's say I had a close call with a driver who cut me off on the highway. Even though there was not an accident, I was scared for an instant and I might have reacted with anger to include making some nasty gestures to the other driver. Chances are that if another driver does the same thing in the future I will become similarly irritated. The initial incident could have left such an impression on me that even if I am just a witness to a similar event happening to another driver, I could have a similar emotional response. The initial incident may have caused a minor injury because the event produced an intense emotional reaction. These types of close calls on the highway, however, are not the type of experiences that would cause me to stop driving altogether. Pet peeves do not have the paralyzing effect that catastrophic traumas do. Most people simply get irritated with the driver that cut them off, wishing that a cop would have been present, to give them a ticket or that he hits the next tree, without dying, and continue driving. The moment I start to show instinctive emotional responses to bad driving, I can say I have a pet peeve.

Pet peeves involve complaints about specific actions, rather than a general dissatisfaction about life. They often revolve around behaviors of people close to us, such as a spouse or significant other. We may have objections to disrespectful language, bad manners, poor personal hygiene, poor people skills, or other minor family issues like leaving your shoes in the living room and leaving dirty dishes on the dining table. These behaviors are not big enough to cause permanent rupture in relationships, but they are irritants that produce enough tension to encourage intense family interactions.

An example of a pet peeve involving disrespect could happen when someone sticks his fork on someone else's plate during dinner. While some people do not object to someone else's fork on their plate, there are many others who find this behavior irritating. That's the nature of pet peeves. They are particular to some individuals while not affecting other people at all.

Pet peeves associated with driving can result in road rage, when the person who feels peeved seeks some sort of retribution for the action. These include forgetting to use the turning signal or crossing from the left lane to take a right exist at the last second, in front of other cars. Many consider road rage itself a pet peeve. Other driving-related pet peeves include drivers who speed up to keep others from changing lanes (gap snatchers), or distracted drivers talking on their cell phones (motor mouths). My wife gets particularly irritated by the texting of motor mouths.

A pet peeve that feels very logical to us would seem illogical or even irrational to others. For example, a supervisor may react angrily if the copier lid is left open. Others would become annoyed if they are interrupted while speaking, or when subordinates leave their desks in disarray. That same supervisors may witness employees coming into work late and not feel any annoyance whatsoever. Pet peeves are only important to the degree that they remind us about uncomfortable personal issues. The next category, which is the main focus of the rest of the book, are the catastrophic spiritual injuries. Let's take a look.

Catastrophic Spiritual Injuries

A ten-year-old boy instinctively believes that his father should be his protector. However, if his father beats him for the flimsiest of excuses, the boy could begin to see his father as his perpetrator. The beatings could become an irreconcilable contradiction that a ten-year-old child does not have the spiritual maturity to reconcile. It is very possible that the lasting effects from his father's physical abuse will develop into a violent response to his own circumstances in school and with friends. The severity of the damage will not be felt for years, but the child's character could be altered to the point of rendering

him incapable of establishing relationships with other people without using violence. The worst aspects of the injury will not be fully manifested until the child is an adult and he also, becomes a father.

Catastrophic spiritual injuries are the result of a highly emotional trauma that leaves a permanent memory (spiritual scar) because of the irreconcilable contradiction they produce. Generally, the trauma is the result of an event that contradicts people's deeply and instinctively held beliefs. In order for an injury to be catastrophic, it must have two components. First, it must be a clearly traumatic event that creates the irreconcilable contradiction. Second, it must cause severe damage to people's ability to establish healthy intimate relationships with others. This type of injury must result in damage to the intimacy mechanism (more on this concept later).

Let me make two additional clarifications. First, the initial pain caused by the traumatic event will subside eventually, but the memory of guilt or shame could remain for years. Most people respond with silence to these shameful and guilt-ridden memories because they cannot afford to talk about those events without experiencing the original trauma as if it had just happened. These traumas become forbidden subjects because speaking about them can disrupt the superficial tranquility of the family unit. This is one of the main reasons children don't speak out when they are abused by a family member or friend. Before long, these types of injuries turn into family secrets that no one, especially the injured person, would dare mention. Second, after the initial pain has subsided the individuals tend to lose the connection between the lingering pain and the injury that caused it. This disconnection has the unintended consequence of lengthening the healing process. When people cannot identify the source of their pain, it becomes more difficult to process the events that caused the spiritual injury, thus making the healing process more difficult.

In this context, an instinctive belief is the normal expression of a deeply held *truth*. This truth is held without debate because it is readily apparent to the individuals holding the belief. For example, most children believe their parents are trustworthy people. This is the reason children run to their parents when they feel any type of fear or danger. Children see their parents as their protectors. This is not

a controversial or difficult concept to accept. This is the reason I say that this type of belief is instinctive. It does not have to be taught. It simply is. When that instinctive held belief is shattered by parental violence against children, the resulting contradiction finds expression through mistrust, resentment, and anger.

The trauma is often the result of persistent abuse or neglect. This type of abuse or neglect normally causes permanent damage to the person's intimacy mechanism affecting how these children relate with others as they grow older. That is, people's ability to sustain healthy intimate relationships is severely impaired when the perpetrator is someone to whom the victim is emotionally attached. Most of us would agree that healthy emotional intimacy is based on trust and respect and when that trust is violated, it becomes more difficult to be vulnerable in relationships. Since the physical and emotional trauma damage the ability to trust, then, establishing healthy relationships is not an actionable option for the injured person. Injured individuals choose to put on a façade that mimics intimacy while resentment continues to bubble up inside their broken hearts. The resulting contradiction creates the need to hide the pain and deny the effects of the trauma, which is nothing more than a survival mechanism. By keeping the event secret, the person's healing process is delayed indefinitely.

Additionally, catastrophic injuries could also cause permanent damage to a person's perception of self. This is especially true in cases of abuse and neglect. In many cases, injured people tend to blame themselves for their suffering. On other cases, the perpetrator manipulates the victim to shift the blame from him to the victim. In both cases, the victim absorbs the perpetrator's guilt and shame adding insult to the injury. With the loss of self-esteem, their relationships with the rest of the world becomes mostly reactive. This means that the person's primary goal turns from seeking healthy intimate relationships into impulsive avoidance of additional pain and further degradation. In this instance, these individuals develop the tendency to view their character and life through the demeaning conditions created by the traumatic event. In most of these cases, the perpetrators add to the pain by manipulating their victims into believing that they, the victims, are to blame for their own victimization. This is the case

when a sexual predator tells his victim that the reason he violated her was because she was too pretty. The net result of the manipulation by the perpetrator and the resulting self-blame is a damaged intimacy mechanism that prevents the person from developing healthy social interactions with others.

Let me summarize some of the symptoms a broken intimacy mechanism reveals. First, there is an erosion in the person's ability to trust others. Second, it produces a sense of shame and guilt that is projected onto other people. Third, it does not allow people to love freely to avoid the risks associated with trusting others. Finally, a damaged intimacy mechanism results in an out of balance expression of feelings.

I can identify two extreme expressions of out of balance feelings. Some people could withdraw from relationships, while others could become clingy or promiscuous. For the withdrawn person relationships are dirty or unnecessarily risky. For the clingy person relationships are almost exclusively defined through sexual intercourse. As a result of this damage, feelings are filtered through the spiritual injury, preventing the person from making impartial assessments in their relational needs. This means that the mistrust, the resentment, and the anger make spiritually injured people more guarded about how, when, and with whom they would establish emotional intimacy. Example: A child that is disciplined exclusively with violence could develop the tendency, as an adult, to discipline his own children with violence. However, if the same children grow up to become so repulsed by the violence they experienced, they may become too tolerant of their own children misbehavior, rendering them impotent to establish healthy disciplinary parameters for their children. Let us take a look at one of the elements that could hinder our ability to heal from spiritual injuries.

The Unchangeable Past

When people are unable to leave the past behind them, their healing process could be delayed for years. I would like to point out that a movement toward spiritual health does not eliminate any already

existing injuries. Since we cannot change the past, we must find a productive method to shift our attention from events we cannot change or remedy, to focus our attention on the future with anticipation and hope. As the saying goes, "we cannot change where we started, but we can influence where we will finish."[4] When we have hope for the future, we can rejoice in the present. Since spiritual injuries leave people with the permanent memory of an event that marked them forever, I call these memories spiritual scars, the key to successful living is to shift our focus from the injury and the pain to a future with hope. This is the reason that when people develop the proper understanding of their spiritual brokenness, they can become proactive in using the trauma as a tool to become better and to succeed in dislodging from the chains of the past. Our spiritual brokenness can lead to faith in God, which can lead us to hope for the future and to restoration for our souls.

Since spiritual injuries are the result of past experiences, and since people cannot undo the past, they need to find healing in the present if they want to move to the future with anticipation and hope. One of the key elements for spiritual healing, therefore, is changing people's focus from being past oriented to becoming future oriented. As long as people are focused on the past, they won't be able to get past the pain produced by the spiritual injury. The transition from being past oriented to future oriented means people have we begun to live by faith. Faith is the one element in the human character that allows us to escape the past by living with hopeful anticipation of the future while learning to live the present without holding grudges or with unresolved resentments. The Bible says that "faith is the substances of the things hoped for and the evidence of the things not seen" (Heb. 11:1). The apostle Paul said the following about his desire to leave his past behind him: "But one thing I do: forgetting what lies behind and straining forward to what lies ahead" (Phil. 3:13b). While faith is built upon God's actions of the past, it's focus is in the hope that God's favor is a promise that will find its ultimate fulfillment in eternity. People can remember the past on their own, but they need to know and believe God's promises to live with anticipation of the future.

---

4   Unknown.

This is one of the reasons the Bible states, paraphrasing, that faith is being sure of what we hope for. Guilt and shame are past focused. They are the results of spiritual injuries that have robbed people of their ability to engage others honest and sincere relationships. Faith is future oriented, which means faith gives people hope, and hope gives them a powerful motivation to live.

All contradictions have to be reconciled, but this can only be done when people regain their standing before God. It is important to note that reconciling the internal contradictions does not mean that people get rid of their brokenness. Rather, reconciliation, in this context, means that people have accepted the reality that a specific event caused a spiritual injury and have found a healthy alternative to manage the subsequent dysfunction. The question is not, how can people get rid of their spiritual injuries? That is not possible. The question is, how can they heal their broken hearts to live with hope and joy? Let us consider God's creation plan for humanity as we try to answer the previous question.

Created in God's Image

Moses described God's creation of Adam and Eve as a two-step process. First, "the LORD God formed the man from the dust of the ground..." (Genesis 2:7a). "The Hebrew text uses here the word *'adam*, which is translated 'man,' and which is related to the word *'adamah*, which means 'ground.'[5] This means that Adam's name was taken from the ground that gave *birth* to him (see Genesis 2:7). The second part of the process is that [God] "breathed into his nostrils the breath of life, and the man became a living being" (Genesis 2:7b).[6] The breath of life is to be understood as "the breath that gives life" or "the breath that causes the man to live."[7] I believe the phrase implies that God created Adam with God's attributes of personhood, such as

---

[5] W. D. Reyburn., & E. M. Fry. (1998). *A handbook on Genesis* (New York: United Bible Societies), p. 63.

[6] Ibid, p. 63.

[7] Ibid, p. 64.

free volition, self-awareness, the capacities to love, to have faith, and to feel empathy for others.

Humanity is, therefore, the merger of the temporal (earthly dust), and the eternal (God's breath.) The phrase that Adam became a living soul is intended to make a distinction between humanity, as a special creation, from animals. Let me note that God had already created animal life, and thus, Adam's creation was not about life itself. It is very possible God also created animals from the dust, but the writer did not make this point. In all likelihood, God made a direct creation of all animals and their capacity to adapt to their environment and reproduce into various forms within the specie. However, when God breathed his Spirit into man, he was creating something unique—a conscious creature that could relate to God as a person. Probably, the best explanation for the distinction between Adam and the rest of the animals in the Garden was that God bestowed man with *personhood* attributes. It is those personhood attributes that distinguish man from animals and connect man to God. God created man with self-awareness and the capacity for conscious and purposeful self-determination. These were essential elements in Adam's creation to fulfill God's desire for a reciprocal relationship between man and God. Of all the divine personhood attributes God gave Adam, freewill (moral freedom) is probably the most significant. Freewill defines people's ability to make free choices, within the limitations of their nature and without external compulsion. Human choices must be free in order for people to be morally responsible and accountable to God for their actions. Otherwise, moral responsibility and accountability would not be possible. For instance, if God had established a deterministic system, people would not be any different than animals that function on hard wired instinct. It is not possible to establish reciprocal and loving relationships with creatures that function on instinct, or that are determined. In Adam, God created a person in his "image and likeness" with whom he could establish intimate and spiritual relationships (Gen. 1:26).

Biblical revelation indicates that animal life and human life are different in kind and scope. While both humans and animals are living creatures, only humans have self-awareness and purposeful intentionality. Does this mean that human life is divine? Yes and no.

Human life is divine in that it has the personhood qualities that are distinctive to God. And no, because people will never be elevated to deity status in that we will never have omniscience, omnipotence, or omnipresence. I believe the phrase "created in God's image" indicates that people have the moral capacity to discern the difference between right and wrong, good and evil. That was Moses's point when he defined the tree at the center of the Garden as the "tree of the knowledge of good and evil" (Gen. 2:16-17).

From God's perspective, people are worthy of his love. Otherwise he would not have created us. Additionally, if God was willing to send Jesus to pay our sin debt, which is death, he must have felt compelled to reveal his love to us in a tangible way. This is true, especially since we can never earn God's love with good behavior. Jesus is God's love gift to us. Love is his motivation to bring us into fellowship with him. Love is the capacity to seek someone else's well-being without expecting anything in return from the object of love. Love provides the foundation for spiritual and emotional intimacy, and intimacy is based on trust. This is the area in which spiritual health is needed. People cannot trust unless or until the intimacy mechanism has been repaired and is working properly. I believe this is the reason God wants to restore his image in us to its original purpose. The first Adam sinned against God and lost his place to live with transparency in God's presence. The "last Adam," Jesus Christ, restored humanity to fellowship with God through his personal sacrifice to pay the penalty imposed by the law of Moses (1 Cor. 15:22, 45).

God's image finds its expression through us when we function in accordance to God's character. For instance, God is love, and we have the capacity to love God and others (1 Jn. 4:16). God is just and we, even in our fallen state, understand both the meaning and practice of justice. He is gracious and merciful, and we have the capacity to show grace and mercy to others. Human life is, therefore, different from animal life in our self-awareness, self-determination, purposeful existence, and in our knowledge of "good and evil." Additionally, since God reveals himself through love, and love is inherently relational, it is imperative that our intimacy mechanism functions properly to relate with God. Not only that, but since God gave us

a deep desire for honest and transparent relationships with other people, it is essential to be open to love others as God has loves us.

When God's image in us is damaged by personal sin (self-inflicted spiritual injuries) or by injustice (spiritual injuries inflicted on us by others), the intimacy mechanism is impaired. This means that a damaged intimacy mechanism cripples people's ability to relate with God and to their neighbor with agape love, which are the two greatest commandments (Lk. 10:27a). In order to have healthy emotional connections with God and other people, people need a healthy self-awareness, which can be identified through a clear understanding of their true worth in relationship to the Creator.

Please understand that since people are both spiritual and physical beings, they cannot completely divorce their emotional experiences from their physical responses and vice versa. This can be clearly seen in people's reactions to snakes or to wild animals. The animal is a physical threat that can produce anxiety, fear, and panic. Often times fear, for example, can produce muscle spasms or intense sweating, which are physical responses to a spiritual or emotional experience.

When Jesus stated, "Love your neighbor as yourself" (Lk. 10:27b), he was making a radical statement. In one simple statement Jesus had given the rationale for spiritual relationships based on a healthy perception of self. It is difficult to imagine how to simplify Jesus's presentation of these two profound principles. Jesus established a distinctively spiritual principle with a testable application on how we relate to others. His premise appealed to our innate drive of self-preservation as a means to draw out our love for our neighbor. Since the Bible also states that God is love, then, loving other people is an extension of God's love for us expressed through self-love. Jesus, then, used the unquestioned truth of self-love as the starting point to draw a direct line from God's love, to self-love, to love for our neighbor. This is an unbreakable continuum.

In other words, Jesus was presenting the human sociological need to develop healthy intimate relationships through the existence of the undeniable principle of loving others as we love ourselves. Let me reiterate the importance of this principle. This is a distinctively relational dichotomy that is made possible by God's love revealed through the person of Jesus Christ. This connection highlights the

need to repair the intimacy mechanism to facilitate the expression of agape love. But it also brings into focus *why* relational brokenness has such a powerful impact on who we are and how we view God and others. Needless to say, when people's intimacy mechanism is damaged through a relational traumatic event, people's ability to express agape love is also diminished. But there is always hope with God.

Since the two greatest commandments are to "love God and to love our neighbor as ourselves," any damage to the intimacy mechanism hinders people's ability to have an emotional connection with God and others, preventing them from enjoying love's ultimate blessings which are healthy intimate relationships with God and people. Let me add that our ability to relate with God and others is an essential element in the spiritual healing process. We cannot heal in isolation. God's ultimate goal is to reconcile us with him and to live in peace with our neighbor. Since God gave us the innate capacity to love self and others, it is unnatural for people to live with hateful attitudes, even though sin and spiritual injuries have distorted God's purpose for our lives. In a very real sense, hatred is a result of sin and not a reflection of who God created us to be. Clearly, if our ability to love ourselves has been damaged, loving others is out of the question. If loving God and loving others is God's ultimate goal, then, repairing the intimacy mechanism is of primary importance to heal the brokenhearted. Therefore, spiritual health means to be restored to God's initial design for humanity which was for people to be in eternal fellowship with him, and to develop transparent relationships with others.

Created With Direct Access to God

The Garden of Eden was intended as a place of rest, communion with God, and, eventually, a place of fellowship with fellow man. God designed the Garden as place in which God could have intimate relationships with Adam and Eve. The first couple did not have any barriers or inhibitions that could prevent their fellowship with God and with each other. Moses wrote that "they were naked and felt no

shame" (Gen. 2:25). The phrase means that Adam and Eve had total access to God and complete transparency with God and with each other. After sin entered their lives, they became ashamed of their very existence and their intimacy with God was severed. When shame enters people's consciousness, the need to hide from God and others is irresistible. As it happened with Adam and eve, people's transparency turns into defensive reactivity. When God came *looking* for the first couple in the Garden of Eden, Adam said to God, "I heard the sound of you in the garden, and I was afraid, because I was naked, and I hid myself" (Gen. 3:10). God asked Adam, "who told you that you were naked?" (Gen. 3:11).

They had disobeyed God when they ate from the tree of the knowledge of good and evil. Ultimately, each one of us wants to get back into the kind of intimacy Adam and Eve enjoyed with God in the Garden of Eden. Since intimacy is based on transparency, and transparency is based on trust, it becomes imperative to regain our ability to trust in order to regain our God given purpose — to engage in healthy intimacy with God and neighbor. Transparency is possible only when we are not driven into hiding from people for shameful behaviors and or attitudes. If we hide from people, we cannot be intimate with them.

At the cross, Jesus dealt with sin which was the underline problem that had brought shame into our lives. Once Jesus dealt with our shame, we became free to reenter into God's presence. God is no longer hidden from us and we do not have to be afraid to enter into his presence. We do not need to pretend that God cannot see us. Jesus's sacrifice on the cross effectively gave us access to the Most Holy Place. The temple had a veil that separated the altar from the rest of the temple. It symbolized the separation that existed between God and us. Only the High Priest could enter the Most Holy Place, and that only once a year. When Jesus died, the veil in the Temple was torn from top to bottom and the Most Holy Place was exposed (Matt. 27:51). The symbolic meaning of the torn veil is that God gave us access to him through Christ. But once Jesus dealt with sin at the cross, men and women received access to God's presence without fear of retribution.

People can begin the reparation process of the intimacy mechanism when they recognize that Jesus dealt with the source of our shame. Once people accept that sin keeps them separated from God, and come to Him with believing hearts, then, they can change the behavior that perpetuates their shame. Finally, people need to accept God's unmerited gift of salvation in Christ to enjoy his presence. Spiritual health, at its core, is the discovery of inner peace in a process of reconciliation with God and other people. The basic point is that people find peace in their relationship with God when they no longer feel ashamed to be *naked* in His presence. Additionally, people find peace in their relationship with other people when they are genuinely interested in their wellbeing.

The Prevalence of Broken Hearts

Most of us have seen our share of brokenhearted people during our lives' journey. Some of us have experienced brokenness in our own hearts. Our shared struggles should help us understand the plight of other people who are also suffering. My brokenness should encourage me to show empathy and compassion for our fellow travelers. The prophet Isaiah predicted that Jesus, who "had been anointed by the Spirit of the Lord," would come to "bind (heal) the brokenhearted, to proclaim liberty to the captives" (Isa. 61:1). Healing the brokenhearted was Jesus's spiritual mission that required him to become one of us. He experienced our physical struggles, and he was tempted like us, so he could empathize with our plight. Jesus did not only come to forgive our sins and bring eternal reconciliation with God, but he also came to set the captives free. This was a captivity of the heart. We had become enslaved to our suffering, and, as a result, we had lost the freedom to love God and others. Oftentimes, we interpret Isaiah's words, exclusively, as a salvation message. While the prophet spoke about salvation, I believe Isaiah had a broader view in mind. Sin had separated us from God, and that was true enough. But our lives had also become marred by the suffering produced by traumatic events that had left us in a great deal of inner turmoil and spiritual pain.

It is not always possible to engage those who are brokenhearted. Our natural instinct is to avoid anyone we suspect that might be hurting. The way we look at it is that our pain is sufficient for us. And we certainly do not want to take upon ourselves someone else's suffering. The struggle for most people is figure out how they can heal sufficiently to be able to assist others in their healing journey. If we recognize our own brokenness, then, we can extend grace and mercy to others who are also struggling like we have. I realize that even if we wanted to, we probably could not care for all those who are spiritually broken. Regardless of the enormity of the task, like the Good Samaritan, the church should consider entering into the process of healing to offer hope to the brokenhearted we find by the side of the road (Lk. 10:25-37). The spiritually injured are everywhere. They work with us. They go to school with us. They dine in the same restaurants, and they attend the same movies. Their broken hearts are well hidden behind the façade of happiness and success, and each one of them has found different coping mechanisms to survive, but under all the pretenses is a heart longing for God's love. The prophet Isaiah said the Messiah would come to heal the brokenhearted (Isa. 61:1). As the church, we are the Body of Christ on earth. We are now called to heal the brokenhearted. We should embrace Christ's healing mission. This is the mission for which the church exists.

The Desires of the Brokenhearted

When the charged nurse called me, she specifically said the patient was on the last stages of his life. He had been suffering from cancer and the infection had spread throughout the entire body and the prognosis was very poor. According to the nurse, the patient would not make it to the morning. I arrived at the patient's bedside around 11:00 p.m. on a Friday night. The patient had become septic with the infection, but even though he was fully awake, he was also in great pain. The patient shared his life story with me until about 2:00 a.m. on Saturday morning. At the end of our conversation, he had two final requests. His first request was unusual, but understandable. He asked my permission to die. Since he saw me as representing God,

he wanted to confess his life to me and to reconcile himself with God before his life came to an end. He said he had lived a full life, and all he wanted was to finish his journey in peace with God.

His second request was a bit more complicated. He told me that he could not die Tuesday. Tuesday was three and a half days away. I asked him why Tuesday, to which he stated that he wanted me to pray that God would allow him to see his daughter one more time before dying. The problem was that his daughter was traveling from Dallas, Texas and she was scheduled to arrive on Tuesday. This request put me in a bind because, if the nurse was correct, he was not going to see the sunrise that morning, and Tuesday was a bridge too far. The man had made peace with God and he was ready to die, but he wanted to have one final moment of reconciliation with his daughter. His request put my faith on the line. I wanted God to grant this man's desire more than anything else in the world but, ultimately, it was not up to me. I gathered my thoughts and prayed that God would extend this man's life until he had the opportunity to say good bye to his daughter.

He thanked me for the prayer, and I stayed until he fell asleep a few minutes later. I left his bedside with the hope that God would extend his life for four more days. As I passed by the nurse station, I asked her again for the man's prognosis. She repeated her first assessment. The patient would not make it through the rest of the night. She was surprised he had made it until that hour. I remember thinking to myself, "He will not die until Tuesday." As I drove home, I understood the man needed to clear the air of any lingering brokenness by reconciling with God and with his daughter. He had done the first part that night but had to wait for the second part for four more days.

I returned to the patient's room on Monday for a few minutes. To my pleasant surprise, the man was still alive. The nursing staff shared their surprised with me that he was still holding on. His daughter had not arrived. On Tuesday around 10:00 a.m. I was in the patient's room when his daughter arrived. I had the privilege of meeting her for a few minutes. Then, I left them alone, so they could spend some time together. Around 2:15 p.m., I received word from the nursing staff that the patient had slipped into sleep and had passed to eternity

in peace. I knew God had honored the man's request to see his only daughter one last time. He was able to say goodbye to her face to face. I can only imagine this man standing before God being grateful that he had granted his final wish. He had asked God for a four-day extension on his life, and God answered his request. This event is one of God's greatest gifts in my life. There are but only a handful of events that are more significant than to witness hope become real in a person's life.

This story represents the two most significant desires of a broken heart: reconciliation with God, and reconciliation with others. These are still the longing of a people who have suffered from spiritual traumas throughout their lives.

CHAPTER 2

The Foggy Field:
Emotional Confusion

It was the fourteenth round of a championship fight (in those days, boxing championships went fifteen rounds). The fighter who had been winning most of the rounds was caught by a surprisingly fast right hand uppercut to the chin. Before he knew what had happened, he was on the canvas with less than ten seconds left in the round. The referee began the count, but the bell rang before he was able to count to ten and the boxer survived the round. The fallen boxer was literally saved by the bell. As the stunned boxer stumbled to his corner, the cameras were focused on him. He had the most painful expression on his face that I had ever seen on a boxer. He had glazy eyes and his head was not stable. The blow had been devastating.

As soon as the boxer sat down, the trainers began to work on him to clear his mind, but nothing was working. He was very groggy, and it was becoming apparent that he would not be able to answer the bell for the final round. As trainers worked on him, the cameras continued to be focused on the boxer's face. The clock was ticking and something had to be done quickly, if he was going to finish the fight. In one of the close-ups to the boxer's face, you could read when the boxer's lip asked his manager, "What round is it?" He asked the question in Spanish, so I was able to read his lips. The blow was so severe that he had forgotten how long he had been fighting. Needless to say, the boxer was not able to answer the bell for the final round and lost the fight by a technical knockout. A severe emotional blow has a similar effect in people's spirits. It produces what I call the *foggy field.*

Spiritual injuries do not occur in a vacuum. Most people experience them in the most familiar contexts such as their homes, places of work, family reunions, communities, and even churches. Very few people actually experience spiritual injuries in unfamiliar settings, but some of those unfamiliar contexts include kidnappings, prisoner of war experiences, or hostage situations. All the above examples fall under the category of catastrophic spiritual injuries.

For the following paragraphs, I will describe and explain the three primary metaphors that describe the aftermath left by the catastrophic spiritual injuries. While these three metaphors provide a rational approach to spiritual injuries, it is not my intention to suggest that every person experiences these areas in the same way. My purpose is to assist people in identifying the process through which they are struggling. I have concluded that most people will experience a variety of these effects, but everyone that suffers a catastrophic spiritual injury will have a period of confusion (the foggy field) and, eventually, they will develop into blind spots. The time a person spends struggling from one category to the next varies from person to person. These categories are not intended to pinpoint every situation. Rather, they are intended to serve as guides through the spiritual injury progression. In the rest of this chapter I will address the three spiritual stages caused by the spiritual trauma: (1) the foggy field stage of confusion, (2) the spiritual scars that mask the restlessness people feel as long as the spiritual injury remains open, and (3) the creation of lies to rationalize the irreconcilable contradiction. I have identified these lies as blind spots.

First Stage of Confusion: The Foggy Field

An expert Alaskan fisherman related to me the story that on many occasions the Alaskan heavy fog on the ocean would make it virtually impossible for most fishermen to navigate their ships back to shore.[8] When a fisherman is trapped in the dense fog, he would blow his boat's horn once for about twenty seconds, and then he waits. If

---

[8]   David Lemarie. Alaskan pastor and amateur fisherman.

there is another boat outside the fog that hears the distress horn, that fisherman would blow the horn of his boat twice for about twenty seconds each to allow the lost fisherman to identify the direction of the sound outside the fog. Once the disoriented fisherman identifies the direction to safety, he heads in that direction to return to the shore.

Dave's story illustrates the three-steps process to escape the foggy field. First, the disoriented fisherman blows his boat's horn as a distress call. Alaskan fishermen have been agreed to this procedure in advance. They must trust that their fellow travelers will honor the agreement and provide them accurate directions. Second, the fishermen wait for the two sounds of any boat within hearing distance that can provide some direction. That is, after the distress called is sent, the disoriented fishermen remain quiet and follow someone else's instructions and directions. Finally, the lost fishermen follow the origin of the sound outside the fog. In this step the fishermen are trusting that the person who blew the horn will honestly lead him to safety. This three-steps process relies on trust. This illustration fits perfectly the process to escape the foggy field caused by severe emotional trauma.

The foggy field is a temporary emotional state of confusion caused by a stunning and an unexpected blow to our belief system. The emotional blow leaves the person disoriented and unable to focus properly. When people experience an emotional blow of this magnitude, they will not know what to do or how to proceed for a short period of time. The confusion and the pain caused by the stunning blow are real. The immediate aftermath of the trauma is the most dangerous stage for people. Any decisions made during this period of time are almost always wrongheaded and unstable. It is imperative for people to avoid making any major decisions soon after they have received the stunning blow. During the initial stages of the foggy field experience, people may think they can make coherent decisions, but the emotional trauma, by its very definition means that they are not strong enough spiritually to tackle the stress produced by the life changing circumstances they may face, like buying a house or moving to another city.

The desire to escape the place where the injury took place is very powerful, but the wisest decision at this time is to do nothing. People need guidance from someone who is outside the foggy field to make decisions until the emotional fog has cleared. The best counsel we can give a person who enters the foggy field is to do nothing without consulting with a trusted friend, family member, or a counselor. These resources are the voices outside the foggy field (the horn in the Alaskan fog) that give them direction. As soon as people have realized they have entered the foggy field, they need to have enough foresight to stop from making any decisions, contact their voice outside the field, and wait until the effects of the stunning blow have subsided.

For example, a man comes to his house and finds a note from his wife that she left with her boss and she is not returning. The man's initial reactions could include anger, denial, and depression. There is no question that this event is a stunning blow to the man's heart, especially if he loves his wife and had no idea that she had been cheating on him with her boss. In this particular case, in addition to entering into the foggy field, he has also suffered the spiritual injuries of abandonment and betrayal. The man experienced three emotional contradictions at the same time, the betrayal, the abandonment, and the infidelity. In all likelihood, these injuries will damage the intimacy mechanism that will eventually turn into blind spots. The moment the husband received the blow of his wife's betrayal, he could have become disoriented and confused. This highly emotional event prevents him from having clear perception of his options. In a moment of blind rage, he could choose to pursue his wife and lover with the intent to harm them. Or he could turn the anger inwardly and make a suicide attempt. Or he could end up in my office devastated and unable to function. He is in the foggy field.

The Alaskan fishermen have something in common with our process to escape the foggy field. They know the code to escape the fog. A healing church that knows the code to help people escape their spiritual foggy field can play a critical role in procuring the spiritual health of the injured individuals. If a church establishes an accountability system based on fellowship and hope, church members could develop the necessary trust to rely on each other during the times of trouble. The church functions as both, a support system for any member that has experienced a traumatic event, and as an accountability partner to encourage transparency in the healing process. As a supporting system, the church takes a non-judgmental attitude to the trauma, and normalizes the suffering. This allows the person suffering the trauma not to feel like an outcast or worse, as someone that deserved the trauma that came to them.

Emotional and Spiritual Paralysis

Rose looked lost. She rambled on for several minutes before I was able to ask what brought her to my office. Her only coherent statement was to say that she was confused. She did not know where she was headed or even if she was making any progress. She just continued with her incongruent conversation. I asked Rose, several times, what had brought her to my office without getting a clear response from her. Finally, I was able to ask her a different set of questions hoping that she could offer some insight into her problem, but she was still not able to give me a clear answer. Rose repeated the same words, "I am just so confused."

It was then I realized that Rose could not articulate why she came to my office because she really did not have a clear picture regarding her thought process. Something had happened to her, but she was truly confused and disoriented, not about the event, but about her response to it. She had entered the foggy field. Rose stayed in the office for another 40 minutes, until she finally agreed to return for counseling and to make no decisions until after we had talked again. Upon her return, Rose was able to articulate the shock she received when her husband suffered a massive heart attack at the age of 42 and died. Rose told me that she always believed she would die before her husband, and she felt he had abandoned her. Rose was not out of the foggy field, but she could now begin her process to grieve her husband and heal.

Several years ago, I read in the newspaper about weather conditions that contributed to a pile-up of over 100 cars on Michigan Highway I-94 on January 9, 2014, near Kalamazoo, Michigan. It was cold and icy, and the fog was so thick that visibility was almost non-existent. Car after car ran into the vehicle just ahead of them. The icy road conditions contributed to the accident, but without the fog, most of those cars would not have ended up on top of each other.

Fog has distinct qualities. Physical fog is clear enough to allow free movement, but it can be thick enough to prevent people from actually knowing where they are going. While in the foggy field, like the cars on the Michigan highway, people lose their sense of direction. They cannot see clear enough to discern the dangers ahead of them. It is necessary to clarify that people in the spiritual foggy field are not irrational. However, their minds have become temporarily confused, like it happened to the boxer mentioned above, and it becomes more complicated to make rational decisions. The thickness of the fog is determined by the severity of the spiritual trauma, and it can prevent individuals from taking proactive actions. Additionally, poor visibility produces the feeling that people are not making progress or that they have lost control. Since the fog (the confusion) looks the same in all directions, people would have a difficult time determining what to do next. This means that people's sense of spiritual direction is temporarily disabled. They need guidance, the proverbial horn from outside the foggy field, to escape.

The spiritual foggy field experience could also result in an emotionally severe blow to people's belief systems. The trauma represents a contradiction to what people instinctively believed. Either, they were unprepared to receive the stunning blow, or the blow was so severe that nothing could have prepared them for the contradictory impact. Any violent act within the family unit could create a contradiction that damages people's belief systems. Children, for instance, believe their parents should be their protectors. If the parents become their tormentors, then, the violence creates a contradiction that puts into question their belief that home is a safe and trusting environment.

Let me add that it is possible to receive a stunning blow that creates a foggy field experience without resulting in a catastrophic spiritual injury. An example of this could be when a church leader falls into sin. The congregation could experience a short period of spiritual confusion until the issues are clarified. Once the congregation has achieved a certain sense of clarity, the fog will disappear, and the church can continue her spiritual mission. However, if the event produces an irreconcilable spiritual contradiction in some of people involved, then, for those individuals, a spiritual injury could develop. In this latter case, the people caught up in the irreconcilable contradiction, could abandon the church, and the most extreme cases, they could even abandon the faith altogether.

Escaping the Foggy Field

A young woman who had attended one of my seminars on spiritual health sent me an email several months later to let me know that she spent eight years in the foggy field. She stated in her email that she could not bring herself to trusting anyone, and that as a result she remained paralyzed in her relationships as well as her job progress and performance. She felt isolated in the midst of an overcrowded world. She stated in her email that the seminar had given her the courage to finally trust someone and to seek counsel with a mentor that could help her escape the foggy field. She told me that four months after the seminar, her mind was clear for the first time since she could remember and for the first time in many years she had renewed hope for her future.

The first order of business is to get out of the foggy field (to get past the initial state of spiritual confusion). Until this is done, all our efforts to heal from the spiritual injury will be severely restricted. People need to regain their rational and emotional perspective to take proactive actions in their healing process. Once they have their thoughts in order (or she has her feelings in order), they can make the necessary decisions for their immediate future. During the foggy field experience, the main concern is not the spiritual injury itself because we still don't know if the emotionally stunning blow has turned into a spiritual injury. There will be plenty of time to work on the contradiction, if any arose, after people have escaped the foggy field and their minds have cleared up.

There are three basic steps to assist people to get out of the foggy field. First, the present emotional state of confusion needs to be normalized. That is, people need to know and feel that their emotional confusion is a perfectly normal reaction to the events they had just gone through. Additionally, they need to know that others understand this state of confusion. Even though the foggy field is very real, people need to know that it is a temporary emotional state of confusion that will eventually subside. The biggest challenge for people in the foggy field is to trust someone on the outside to guide them out of this spiritual state of confusion. In this first step, the goal is to calm people down by reassuring them that their experience is normal, but that it is also temporary. When we normalize the confusion, we are encouraging the person not to dwell on the event that sent them into the foggy field. Rather, we want the traumatized person to understand that their struggle is normal, and as such, there is a solution.

Second, people need to understand *why* they have the hopeless feeling of being trapped without options. Hopelessness is the result of impaired insight (limited spiritual vision). This means that people cannot see beyond their present circumstances, and as a result, they are unable to find options to remedy their situation. The empty feeling of being without options to remedy the present predicament intensifies their sense of hopelessness. If people cannot visualize an end to the foggy field, they could feel trapped in this emotional confusion created by the stunning blow for an extended period of time.

During these intense periods of confusion, people feel they are unable to make any progress. They need to be reassured that this is a temporary condition produced by the stunning emotional blow they had just received. The most immediate need for the person in the foggy field is to find a trustworthy voice within the first few days of the emotional trauma that can assist them to walk out to safety. Once people accept the legitimacy of the feelings of confusion, they can eliminate the stigma brought about by the fears associated with the event. If people are able to accept their feelings as normal, the chances of regaining hope increase. They need to know they are not losing their minds. The validation of their feelings allows them to take the first critical step to escape the foggy field to regain inner composure.

Finally, people need to find the courage to trust someone outside the foggy field. They need an accountability partner. This is the proverbial Alaskan horn that provides guidance to disoriented fishermen. Trust in a person outside the fog is critical to speed up the process to get out of the state of confusion. Trust gives the person the confidence they need to follow the voice outside the foggy field. This is often very difficult to do because these people have just experienced severe emotional trauma that has negatively affected their ability to trust other people. This possibility makes it imperative to choose their voice before the traumatic experience knocks on their door. In other words, people need to establish healthy accountable relationships before they have to face the foggy field by themselves.

Once the trauma has occurred, their choices to trust others are limited. Nevertheless, they must gather enough courage to trust the voice outside the foggy field for guidance and direction to escape the initial effects of the trauma. The traumatized person needs clarity in their thinking, and the voice outside the foggy field becomes their spiritual safety net. However, in order for the safety net to achieve its goals, the voice outside the field has to be a trustworthy friend or a spiritual advisor. Accountability partners provide guidance until the traumatized person has regained a clearer perspective of what they have experienced. The voice gives them a sense of direction, which is our most pressing need.

The first two statements are diagnostic in nature. The third statement is to encourage trust and accountability. Trust allows the person to listen to the voice outside the foggy field. Accountability encourages the injured person to avoid decisions until after they have consulted with a trusted friend. Without trust, communication will be a hit-and-miss exercise. And without accountability, people do not know if they are applying the learned principles properly. The initial progress will be slow and tedious. However, as people get closer to the end of the foggy field, they develop more confidence in the voice and in their ability to overcome the symptoms of the initial trauma.

When people are in the foggy field, they have two courses of action. As mentioned earlier, the first course of action is to find someone outside the foggy field they can trust to guide them to safety. They need to stay with that person until they their minds have cleared up and the fog has been listed. Trusting someone is a particularly difficult thing to do. Since many, if not most, of the foggy field experiences are the result of trauma caused by people in our inner emotional circle, trusting someone is a prohibitive option, at best. Nevertheless, if the person is going to escape the foggy field, they must trust someone disconnected to the events to guide them out.

Second, people who have experienced a traumatic event need to avoid life changing decisions. Chances are that making any decision during the foggy field state of mind could bring regrets later. These decisions may, in fact, push people deeper into the fog of confusion. At this stage of the process, following and being accountable to the voice outside the foggy field is the most sensible and prudent option.

There is an additional problem for people who could are in a foggy field experience. If by the time the trauma takes place that creates the state of confusion, they do not have anyone they can trust, it would become extremely difficult to trust someone after the traumatic event. This inability to trust could delay the process of escaping the foggy field, as the young lady I mentioned earlier who spent eight years trapped in this state of confusion. It is critical for people to develop enough friendships before any trauma takes place so that they can have a trusted voice if a spiritual injury were to occur.

However, if these individuals have already lost trust in God and others, the healing process becomes more complicated. The injured person must relearn how to trust someone else and this could take time—and time is not a friend to the person in a deep state of emotional confusion. Trauma requires prompt attention. It is very likely that by the time people receive the full impact of a stunning blow as an adult, they would have already suffered minor spiritual injuries that could have eroded their trust in God and others. Obviously, the greater the loss of trust before the traumatic event takes place, the more difficult it becomes to find an exit from the foggy field. For those who have already suffered the loss of trust, allow me to share several suggestions.

The first suggestion is preventive in nature. People need to identify, as soon as they are able, whether they have trust *issues*. If this is the case, they need to take steps to identify the reasons for their loss of trust. Once they have identified the problem, they can begin to isolate the events that might have eroded their ability to trust. That is, isolating the causes that produce their trust issues help them avoid making unnecessarily broad generalizations that hinders their ability to trust others. In other words, the only person I should not trust at this time is the one who caused my spiritual injury. They should not project their trust problem onto the rest of the world. Let me reiterate that the inability to trust is an indication the intimacy mechanism has suffered damage as a result of previous spiritual injuries, even if they were not catastrophic in nature. Once they accept that their intimacy mechanism is damaged, or that they have trust issues, then, they can take proactive measures to trust again. Without trust, people have the tendency to become isolated, which is what happens in the foggy field. If people wait for the next traumatic event to start working to regain trust, they could struggle more than they are prepared to manage.

The second suggestion is that people should settle down on some basic spiritual principles that could allow them to take emergency steps to manage the trauma while waiting for outside help. In the event of an extreme spiritual trauma and emotional disturbance, those basic skills could be the difference between a speedy escape from the foggy field and a prolonged journey. When those necessary life skills are absent, people could be forced to make some of the most drastic decisions they have ever made at a time they are the least prepared. People would be required to muster the courage to trust someone they would not normally trust.

However, if neither of these suggestions is viable, then, people need to accept that the foggy field experience could extend much longer than it needs to be. After the stunning blow has produced the initial confusion, the road to exit the foggy field without an outside help will not be an easy one. Sooner or later, people need to begin trusting again, even if it's just enough to escape the confusion. Otherwise, the emotional confusion turns healing into a prolonged and unpredictable process.

The Foggy Field for Men and Women

The most obvious statement is that men and women experience the foggy field differently. The state of confusion created by the trauma is similar, but the source of mistrust and anxiety originates from different areas of their psyche. Men's state of confusion comes when they experience a flood of feelings. Since men filter most of their issues through logical reasoning (regardless of how logical their thinking actually is), a flood of feelings would create spiritual confusion and paralysis. Of course, this is not to say that men do not have feelings—they do. This is to say that when men receive an emotionally charged blow, they have to find a logical explanation for the event, or deep confusion will ensue. Most men are not able to process their experiences through feelings. Feelings confuse men until they grow to recognize that feelings are a natural response to events and people. When men experience a stunning blow, they make statements from logic such as: "There is no reason for her to leave me after all I have done for her." Or, "I was making the adjustments she had asked me." These logical statements are an attempt to bring sanity to his emotional chaos. The role of the voice outside the foggy field is to help men clarify the feelings from a logical perspective. The best step is to normalize the man's emotional confusion.

Women, on the other hand, handle feelings very well. They become confused when they are flooded with logic. Again, this is not to say that women are illogical. Rather, this means that women's first response to any situation is from a feelings perspective as oppose to a logical one. If the husband leaves his wife and gives her a logical explanation like, "I am leaving you because you are unwilling to stop nagging me," he will confuse her. The husband is trying to give her a logical explanation to what he perceives is his wife's disrespectful attitude. The husband thinks that his wife's nagging makes him feel dumb. Since the wife processes her experiences emotionally, her answer to her husband would likely be a statement disconnected to her husband's original charge, like, "Oh, yeah, and your mother stinks." This is not an indication that the wife is not logical. Rather, it is an indication that she has lost her point of reference to properly understand the husband's logical explanation. If the husband had said: "I feel disrespected when you talk down to me," the wife would have a clearer point of reference. The woman would understand an explanation based on feelings better than the explanation based on logical reasoning. Again, this is not to say that women are illogical, or that men do not feel. Rather, this is to say that when they are flooded with logic-driven arguments women could become temporarily confused.

Allow me one clarification. Women can be as logical as men when they are not flooded with logic, and men can be as emotional as women when they are not flooded with feelings. The flood of logic (for women) or of feelings (for men) creates confusion because the relational starting point is different for men and women.

Second Stage of Confusion: Spiritual Scars

In November 28, 1978, around 11:45 a.m., I was running the army's Jungle Expert Training obstacle course. It had been raining since very early in the morning, and the course was wet and slippery. I navigated the first three obstacles without difficulties. However, the fourth obstacle was particularly difficult. We had to climb up a palm tree using a rope, do a monkey crawl on a rope bridge with our rucksacks and rifles on our backs. Then, we had to climb down on another rope attached to a second palm tree. I had done this exercise countless times, but this day, as I was near the second palm tree and I let go of my right hand to reach for the rope to start going down, my other hand came loosed and my feet slipped off the rope bridge. In a split second, I was falling head first from about fourteen feet high. I stretched my arms to break my fall, but I was carrying too much weight on my back, and when I hit the ground, my right elbow turned the wrong way. The fall shattered the bone near my elbow and dislocated my wrist and shoulder.

The injury required emergency surgery. The surgery was a total success, and I spent nine days in the old Gorgas Hospital in Panama City, Panama. I found out after surgery that the doctors could not repair the bone and had to cut about one inch of the radial bone. Today, more than forty years later, the scar is still visible on my right elbow. It serves as a reminder of the painful accident. The elbow does not hurt anymore, but the memory of the event cannot be erased. The fact is that I fell fourteen feet from a rope bridge carrying a 40 lbs. rucksack. I also lost about a half inch of the radial head bone in my elbow that can never be restored. With plenty of exercise, my elbow became stronger, and while it will never be 100%, I can function fairly well in spite of the injury. However, both the memory of the accident and the results are permanent. I have overcome the pain and do not live my life thinking about that event, but I still remember the exact time of the accident. The accident left a physical mark in me, a scar from the surgery, but it also left a spiritual scar in the form of fear of heights. However, the injury does not dictate how I live my life. Similarly, recovering from spiritual injuries has two main objectives. First, we want to overcome the pain, and second, we want to live beyond the dysfunction caused by the spiritual injury. We need to accept that the spiritual scars (painful memories) will remain, but the actual pain associated with the injury does not have to.

Physical scars are inferior reparations on the skin that do not change the injury's condition. I have a scar on my right elbow that indicate the surgery has healed. This means I am not bleeding from it and I am not in terrible pain as a result of the fall. But I am still missing an inch of the radial head on my elbow. Similarly, spiritual scars generally appear before the individuals have dealt with the consequences of the emotional trauma. This is a necessary result because the first order of business for the injured person is getting rid of the pain caused by the injury. The scars are the mark that the pain caused by the trauma has subsided. But they are also a reminder that the trauma took place. One of the dangers of scars is that they hide the injury leaving the impression that everything is well. As a result, people could lose their ability to recognize the source of the pain, precisely because the scars cover the laceration caused by the event. In other words, the scar makes the real injury invisible because it gives the appearance that the pain has naturally gone away. At this stage of the process, addictive behaviors become a real option to soothe a pain that is no longer connected to a particular injury because the scar has covered it up.

Why is overcoming the pain so important? As most of us know, whenever we experience physical pain, we have difficulties concentrating on anything else. Depending on the pain's intensity, it may actually render the person non-functional. I have suffered from migraine headaches for years. Most of the time I was able to work through the headaches with little or no medication. But from time to time, the headaches were so severe that it became almost impossible to be in a lighted room. I knew exactly where the pain was located, and there was nothing I could have done to stop it. All I could do was wait until the body made the necessary adjustments until the headaches went away.

When people suffer spiritual pain, they will experience similar reactions. As long as the spiritual pain is controlling their every thought, they cannot move past it. When the pain begins to subside, and their minds become clear again, they are no longer in the foggy field of spiritual and emotional confusion. By the time the pain has subsided and the person has escaped the foggy field, the spiritual scar has formed. Eliminating the pain allows the person to regain a more active and congruous lifestyle, even if the spiritual scar continues to be a reminder of the event that brought about all the pain.

Spiritual scars are the visible evidence that both kinds of injuries, superficial and catastrophic, have occurred. Eventually, catastrophic injuries will turn into blind spots when the person develops instinctive compulsive reactions to any situation that may remind them of the pain caused by the original injury. The superficial injuries could become pet peeves, as discussed earlier. Blind spots are a hindrance to the healing process because people's instinctive defensiveness prevents them from actually dealing with the injury. Blind spots, as byproducts of spiritual injuries, are often the cause of the most dysfunctional relationships. Regardless of how serious an injury might be, physical or spiritual, the severity of people's reactivity or blind spots will determine the level of emotional pain associated with it. While I have made reference to physical injuries from the perspective of the physical scars left behind, there is no question that people cannot divorce physical injuries from their emotional responses to them. We are both physical and spiritual beings, and we will always have emotional responses to physical injuries. This is the reason that a fall, such as the one I experienced in the Panamanian jungle, created in me fear of heights.

Once the pain caused by the catastrophic injury has subsided and all that remains is the memory of the injury (the spiritual scar), then the resulting blind spot is virtually impossible to identify without intervention. For instance, children in a family can easily describe their parents' divorce without knowing how this event could impact them in the future. Or a young boy who is constantly rejected for participating in school sports can recognize the rejection, but may not be able to know how the irreconcilable contradiction of his rejection becomes a spiritual injury that can have a negative effect in his ability to trust people around him. Spiritual scars are always connected to the trauma that produced them, even when people are not able to link their emotional reactions to any particular event. People can begin the process to connect the initial injury and the subsequent spiritual scar when they are able to identify their tendency to overreact to common and non-threatening events.

We have already established that most people can identify the events that caused their spiritual injuries. The problem is that most people are not able to connect their present instinctive reactions to a particular spiritual injury. They assume that they have always been this way. This is who they are, but they do not realize that the spiritual injury has conditioned them to choose dysfunctional behaviors. Their emotional reactivity to anything that reminds them of the trauma must be immediately rejected. People's inability to make the connection between their present dysfunctional behaviors and their spiritual injuries delays the healing process indefinitely. Since people do not know how the original event may have affected their characters, they do not know how to correct the resulting crippling dysfunctions. Thus, recognizing their dysfunctional reactions to events and people is a necessary step in connecting the spiritual injury to its source. Making the connection between reactive behaviors to everyday events and the original source of the pain brings us closer to the healing we desperately need.

Spiritually injured people remember their injuries very well. They remember the event, the pain, and the agony they felt when they were going through the experience that damaged them. However, most people cannot identify the reasons they are hurting as adults. They know they have compulsive and addictive tendencies, but they do not know how, or why, their need for self-medication developed. They have defensive reactions to people, but since they have not healed, they can't connect their reactions to their pain. Until the pain has completely subsided, people may resort to self-medication to temporarily sedate the pain. Whenever we see people with compulsive and self-destructive tendencies, we can safely assume that a deeply seated spiritual injury is a contributing factor. Physical injuries, for the most part, have identifiable cures. But spiritual injuries require more than a simple trip to the pharmacy before the person can experience relief.

In the last chapter, we will expand on the healing process, but suffice it here to say that God designed us to live in a community of faith. It is in that community of faith that true spiritual healing takes place. The healing community (the church), is the spiritual support group dedicated to worshiping together, praying for one another, and preaching the message of the gospel—that God's love has been poured out on our behalf through and in the person of Christ. Forgiveness, redemption, and restoration are the hallmarks of a healing community. The church is the place in which people can be restored to fellowship with God to a lasting peace in their souls. We need counselors, pastors, and others who can address the spiritual needs in our lives. This is the reason the apostle Paul said that, "He who descended is the one who also ascended far above all the heavens, that he might fill all things. And he gave the apostles, the prophets, the evangelists, the shepherds and teachers, to equip the saints for the work of ministry, for building up the body of Christ" (Eph. 4:10-12).

Most physical injuries do not leave permanent spiritual scars and, as such, they do not contribute to altering people's characters. But we need to recognize that some physical injuries, like chronic back problems, amputations, cancers, and the like, not only have crippling physical effects, they also condition the way we think about ourselves and the world around us. As mentioned earlier, when physical injuries or illness produce a highly emotional response, then it also becomes part of the person's spiritual makeup. As mentioned earlier, Joni

Eareckson Tada became a quadriplegic at a very young age. And yet, she has dedicated her entire life to bringing hope to people that have suffered in a similar way as she has. Joni has lived an exceptional life. Her crippling physical accident gave her a heightened compassion for people who have been handicapped by physical injuries. Without her own suffering, she probably would not have become the woman of God she became, and she would have lived a much different life. But God took the accident that turned Joni into a quadriplegic and turned her into a ministering, transforming agent to people all over the world.

Since God created us as a unit that contains both physical and spiritual components, we cannot experience the physical world without having a spiritual reaction and vice versa. When people's spiritual and emotional elements are permanently affected by injuries, they will experience changes that become part of their consciousness. They begin to function based on their new reality, even though the blind spots developed subconsciously because they were not fully aware how the spiritual injury had altered their characters. Knowing that all injuries have the potential to influence a person's spiritual make-up allows them to identify the injuries that have, in fact, left a character-defining quality in them. The next step, related to spiritual scars is to make an inventory.

Spiritual Scars Inventory

We need to make an inventory of all our spiritual scars (the memories of spiritually damaging events) to begin the process of connecting our reactivity, defensiveness, and compulsivity with the deeper problems that have caused them. Whenever one of the previous character qualities is present, it is very likely that a spiritual scar is present. And spiritual scars always point to a blind spot that point to a spiritual injury.

The spiritual scars inventory process is simpler than it appears on the surface. People should list any event that, in spite of the number of years that have passed, still remains fresh in their memories. My personal example is the accident in Panama. My fall on the obstacle course is as fresh in my memory today as it if had happened yesterday. In making the inventory, do not leave any events out. The exact time or the precise location of a particular event is not as important as long as we can describe the event itself. However, the more detailed and specific our description, the greater the impact the event had on our character formation. Once we have identified as many events as we can remember, then we can proceed to connect the spiritual scars to the emotional marks a particular event might have left. The more we know about the emotional connection to a particular event (whether physical or emotional), the easier it becomes to identify whether the event created an irreconcilable contradiction, which is the key element to identify spiritual injuries, which is our ultimate goal.

The length of the spiritual inventory process depends on individual circumstances. If in addition to the emotional pain, the event also produced guilt and or shame, then the inventory process could become more difficult. People suffering from guilt and shame are more reluctant to confront the events that produced them. I met a woman who took twenty-six years before she was able to speak out loud that she had been raped when she was seventeen years old. Her shame was so profound that she claimed to have forgotten the event itself. The idea of sharing the event with someone else was not an option for her. She had buried the memories of the event, but when confronted with symptoms that were consistent with some form of sexual trauma, she remembered the event very well. But she had done a magnificent job burying the memories, until she could not hide them anymore. The spiritual scars inventory is a critical initial step for people who are interested in healing.

Taking the inventory is not the end of the process, but it's essential to reveal ignored and hidden memories that have caused anxiety and pain. Another benefit of the inventory is that it can also reveal positive memories that could have played a role in overcoming some of the more painful memories. Just because an event left a permanent mark does not mean it is a spiritual injury. A positive response to a positive event can have a character altering result, but these positive events do not have a negative character altering result that become blind spots. As such, these positive and permanent memories are not spiritual injuries. They don't leave spiritual scars and do not create blind spots.

My wife and I were married thirty-nine years ago. This is a great memory for us. There was a tropical rain mist on that summer day in Puerto Rico. It was a beautiful day. Our wedding has left a permanent positive mark in our souls, but this mark is not a spiritual scar because there is no reactivity and or compulsivity associated with this event. Positive events cannot become spiritual injuries because they do not produce the side effects associated with traumatic events such as the confusion of the foggy field, the denial of the spiritual scars, and the creation of emotional lies.

Once people have identified the events that are most likely the source of the spiritual pain, they can start dealing with the debilitating effects left by the injury. When people suffer from headaches, they would probably take an over-the-counter medication and soon after the headache is gone. Spiritually injured people have the tendency to turn to self-destructive behaviors to provide relief for the pain. The pattern for self-destructive or dysfunctional behaviors is fairly predictable. Until we develop over-the-counter drugs for the soul, most people will choose to self-medicate with addictive substances and behaviors, and they will need spiritual intervention.

If brokenhearted individuals resist the temptation for self-medication, the lingering frustration often finds expression in anger or depressive moods. If they fall into self-medication, then, the addictive behavior becomes a priority and the addiction will block any progress toward spiritual healing. At this point, they would have compounded their spiritual restlessness with a chemical or emotional dependency. The addiction will replace the need to heal the original spiritual injury with the need to get the next fix from the drug of choice. The original pain has not gone away, which is the reason they became addicted in the first place. It has simply been replaced with the new pain caused by the addiction.

By the time the instinctive reactions appear, most of the pain associated with the trauma, that caused the injury, would be lost in the person's subconscious. Spiritual scars, like physical scars, create the illusion that the injury has healed. The appearance of spiritual scars is an indication the defense mechanism is working, and people can move on with their lives, even if some of the original issues remain. The issue now becomes identifying the reactive responses to people and circumstances to determine if the event produced a spiritual injury, or if we are dealing with a superficial injury that, at worst, would become a pet peeve.

It is important to clarify that not all catastrophic spiritual injuries lead to the nearest neighborhood drug dealer to buy the desired over-the-counter drug to alleviate the pain. But, I can say with confidence that addictions, almost always, point to an unresolved contradiction produced by a traumatic event. The drugs of choice include alcohol, cocaine, heroin, and sex, among others. These are easily accessible.

It is my belief that addictions are nothing more than attempts to cope with the unbearable and yet unidentified spiritual pain that cannot be controlled. It is a mistake to label people as weak or evil for their struggle with addictions. Rather, they are emotionally and spiritually sensitive to the pain that drives them. In most cases, when the injury is discovered early enough, people can make full recovery very quickly. However, in some instances, a person could sink so deeply into the world of addiction that nothing can be done until after intense drug rehab treatment. In many instances the addiction leads to death. It has been reported that opioid addiction was responsible for more than 52,000 accidental deaths in 2015 alone.[9] That's almost the same number of deaths in one year compared to the casualties during the thirteen years of the Viet-Nam war. This is how pervasive spiritual injuries have become in the American society. People suffering from addictive behaviors do not need an accusatory finger. They need compassion and care. In many cases, the addiction has become the sole purpose for their lives. When people reach this point, they need to spend some time in a treatment facility to heal from their addictions before we can manage their broken heart. This is when people have reached rock bottom, and the time to escape is at hand.

---

[9] Rudd RA, Seth P, David F, Scholl L. Increases in Drug and Opioid-Involved Overdose Deaths — United States, 2010–2015. MMWR Morb Mortal Wkly Rep 2016;65:1445–1452. DOI: http://dx.doi.org/10.15585/mmwr.mm655051e1

Third Stage of Confusion: Believing a Lie

Randall was a very successful military officer. He was number one in his graduating class. He served a successful tour as a company commander during the Gulf War in 1991. Randall was selected for promotion to Major ahead of his peers, and then he was selected for promotion for Lieutenant Colonel ahead of his peers again. Additionally, he had been selected to be a battalion commander. This selection meant that Randall was on his way to becoming a general officer in the United States army. Any military officer would have loved to have achieved half of what Randall had done. And yet, there he was in my office an alcoholic on the brink of losing everything.

As we chatted, I realized Randall had believed a lie for most of his life that had caused an irreconcilable contradiction in his soul. Randall was not abused, abandoned, or neglected growing up. He grew up in a good home with his two parents, and yet he had an irreconcilable contradiction that had driven him to drown his sorrows in the bottle. After a few sessions, Randall told me that he had believed the lie that *the man* would not allow him to succeed. When I asked him who was *the man*, Randall told me that his grandfather had told him, all his life, that a black man like him could not succeed in a white man's world. And there he was, as one of the most successful officers I had ever seen in all my years of military service, and I had seen many, unable to control his alcoholism. I asked him how he could believe his grandfather's words in light of his own personal experiences of success? He could not answer. Then, it occurred to me that Randall needed to overcome his grandfather's well-intentioned but false words, with his own reality. I asked him to go home that night and write as many events in his life as he could remember that most people would consider a success.

The next day Randall came back to the office with ninety-three successful events. I then asked him, what is the truth? He said: The truth is that I am a very successful man. I then asked him, what is the lie? He said: The lie is that a man like me cannot succeed in a white man's world. I asked him again to restate the truth in light of his lifelong successes. He then said, "The truth is that a black man like me can succeed in a white man's world." And believe it or not, with this simple exercise Randall found freedom from his contradiction and could look at the future with hope.

The third consequence of spiritual injuries is the creation of lies that provide a rationalization for the contradiction. These lies can be the result of an innocent misunderstanding, like the one Randall believed. Regardless of the source of the lie, they have to be replaced with people's existential truth. Jesus proclaimed that "knowing the truth sets people free" (Jn. 8:40). If this is true, then, the opposite is also true. That is, believing lies enslaves people. I believe people have to replace the lies they have believed all their lives with God's truth. The truth has transforming power through the renewing of people's minds (Rom. 12:2).

In Randall's case, the lie had created a congruency gap so wide that he had created a whole conspiracy theory against himself. In his mind, *the man* had predetermined his downfall and there was nothing he could do to stop it, even though he was not aware of any such conspiracy. Randall lived with his grandfather's *lie* most of his life. The reality was that *the man* does not exist, and if he did, he would not care who Randall was. The proverbial man did not know Randall or care about him because *the man* is a figment of the imagination to excuse or explain cultural or personal failures. Besides, in the scheme of things, who is Randall that *the man* must stop him from being successful? Randall created a phantom and then lived in fear of it most of his life. The spiritual injury found expression in the lie, and it was reinforced by Randall's self-fulfilling prophecy to ensure that his lie became his reality.

In the next chapter I will deal with blind spots which are the third area of confusion as a result of spiritual injuries. I give blind spots a full chapter because of the significant role they play in hiding our dysfunctions. They are invisible areas in our understanding that blind people to their own reactions, defensiveness, and temptations.

CHAPTER 3
Blinds Spots: Instinctive Reactivity

When we walked into the Chrysler dealership, all we wanted was to buy a used minivan. During the 1980s, minivans were rapidly becoming the family vehicle of choice for couples with two or more children. Iris and I qualified. We had four children. The salesman went out of his way to point out that one particular minivan, the Dodge Caravan, was a very safe vehicle because the manufacturer had minimized the vehicle's blind spots. Initially, his words did not make a significant impression on me (outside the fact that we ended up buying the van). However, as we drove off, I began to ponder the salesman's statement. This particular minivan model was a safer vehicle because it gave the driver a wider view of the road and of approaching vehicles from both sides of the road. I knew about vehicles' blind spots. After all, I had been driving since I was sixteen. Nevertheless, I found the salesman's statement helpful. It made perfect sense to me. I got it: "This particular minivan is safer because it has smaller blind spots."

Definition of Blind Spots

A blind spot in a car is an area around the vehicle that hides oncoming traffic from the driver's rearview mirrors. Obviously, blind spots in cars make the road more dangerous. However, they are not as dangerous as driving while ignorant of the fact that vehicles have blind spots. The good news for drivers is that they can remedy the situation. Drivers can take proactive steps to protect themselves by identifying where the blind spots are located around their vehicle. Once drivers have identified their blind spots, all they have to do is glance to the area of the blind spots before making turns. As it often happens, I began to look for a spiritual application for the blind spots metaphor. For years I kept the salesman's words tucked away.

God created us with at least one built-in deficiency: we are not omniscient. We cannot anticipate every possible option to events or life's circumstances because we do not have exhaustive knowledge to evaluate all the variables that contribute to an event. Our limited knowledge leaves us blinded to many areas in our lives because we cannot see them or anticipate their outcomes. Most of our mistakes in relationships, business, church leadership, etc., can be traced back to insufficient information, immaturity, or to the blind spots we have developed throughout our lives. We need to come to terms with the fact that we can never have exhaustive information about any of the decisions we make.

There are two additional items we need to keep in mind. First, we need to accept that blind spots are real. We ignore them to our peril. Second, we need to be intentional about reducing their influence over our decision-making process or our instinctive reactions to people or circumstances. We can reduce the negative effects of blind spots by gathering as much information as possible before jumping to any conclusions. We can also recognize that our initial reaction to any issue, would likely be the wrong one.

Blind spots represent the fourth stage of the spiritual injuries' process. They create an emotional vacuum (an empty space) in people's subconscious that hinders their ability to be proactive in responses to people and circumstances. This concept is of such importance that I will use the next chapter to expand on the effects of blind spots. I will focus on the four main areas that are symptomatic of blind spots: (1) behavioral reactivity, (2) false guilt, (3) false shame, and (4) lack of transparency.

Rick asked me if I would consider conducting his wedding ceremony. As a military chaplain, we would conduct weddings for soldiers in our units all the time. This was not a special request. Rick appeared to be in a rush to get married. As I do with everyone who asks me to conduct a wedding ceremony, I asked Rick if he had been married and divorced before. He was young, but it is important to ask the question so that we don't get involved in marrying someone who might still be married. This is against the law. Rick's answer surprised me. He said, without flinching, that he had been married four times and he had divorced four times. Incredulous regarding his answer, I asked him how old was he? He said he was twenty-four years old. My surprise turn into astonishment. If we assume that he married for the first time at twenty, this would mean that Rick's marriages, on the average, had lasted less than a year each.

I told Rick that, unfortunately, I could not perform his wedding because there was a problem with the multiple marriages and divorces, and he was the common denominator. He needed to do a psychological evaluation to find out what made him susceptible to having so many broken relationships. There was no doubt in my mind that Rick had a relational blind spot that made him fall in relationships that were doomed to fail. It is possible that he was unlucky. It was possible the girls were all bad wives. But in all likelihood, the problem was that Rick had experience a catastrophic spiritual injury that had severely damaged his intimacy mechanism. He had a blind spot so large, you could have driven a semi-truck through without him noticing. Rick wanted to love and be loved, but he did not know how. I encouraged him to find answers for his many failures in relationships before pursuing this marriage. I told him that if he really wanted to have a good relationship with this girl, he needed to find out what caused the previous divorces. I never saw Rick again.

Recognizing Blind Spots

Spiritual blind spots are an empty area in our consciousness that prevents us from making sense of a situation that causes fear and pain. They are invisible emotional pockets in a person's spirit. Blind spots are, basically, vacuums of insight. People with relational blind spots will always be in a struggle to develop healthy intimacy with others. The main reason for this difficulty is that relational blind spots often manifest themselves as inability to trust others.

Another issue with blind spots is that people are not always able to connect this vacuum of insight to the original spiritual injury. However, if they are able to identify any of the various character altering elements, they can identify the presence of a blind spot. And once they have identified the presence of a blind spot, they can be sure a character altering spiritual trauma took place at some point in the person's life. At this stage of people's struggle, the emotional pain is the open window to the event. They still don't know which spiritual injury caused a particular blind spot, but now they would have a starting point to address the dysfunctional and self-destructive behaviors.

The apostle Paul suggested that growing in love could be the key to solve this spiritual relational vacuum. Listen to his words: "I pray that your love would grow more and more in knowledge and depth of insight" (Phil. 1:9 NIV). While the disconnection between the pain and the injury makes it difficult to understand the instinctive reactions to events and people, it does not negate that an injury exists. On the contrary, the presence of the instinctive reactions is a good indicator that a catastrophic event created the irreconcilable contradiction in our souls, even when they are not aware of it.

The individual does not need to associate the pain with a specific event to know that an injury in fact has taken place. The presence of the pain is itself an indicator that the injury exists. The pain could be the result of something as simple as experiencing rejection in a business venture. For example: suppose someone rejects a business opportunity solely because they "do not like sales." They are actually saying that they would rather not succeed in this business than to experience the pain of rejection. In other words, if the price for success requires any form of rejection, they are unwilling to pay it. This fear of rejection is especially significant if the pain they fear reminds them of the original injury in which they were rejected by loved ones. People can overcome the fear of rejection when the alternative fear is greater. Anyone interested in growing in a particular area of his life should consider, at least, two alternatives. They can ignore the pain and plow through to their goals in spite of their fears. The reader needs to know that it's difficult to overcome fear and pain at the same time. Or, people can discern the source of the pain and take proactive action against the reactivity created by the blind spot.

Instinctive Reactions

Allow me to share a three-step process that can assist us in identifying and managing blind spots. The most practical way to discover the presence of a blind spot is to detect consistently reactive or defensive emotional responses to people and situations. Reactive and defensive responses are the first indicator that a spiritual scar is present. The importance of the spiritual scars is that they always indicate that either a blind spot or a pet peeve is present. The difference between the blind spots and pet peeves has to do with the intensity and the frequency of the reactive responses. Knee jerk defensiveness is an additional indicator that we are dealing with a blind spot. When individuals have identified any instinctive reactive behaviors, they can move to identify the similarity of the situations that cause the reactions. Most people are not even aware of their defensive and instinctive behaviors. In many instances, they need a friend to identify the behavior before the person has the opportunity to make any healthy corrections to it. Having knowledge of the types of situations that provoke these reactive reactions provides us with the opportunity to become more proactive and less reactive.

For example, let us assume that I become reactive or defensive whenever people call into question my qualifications as a preacher. Before I jump to any conclusions, I should consider whether the claim is true. If it is true that I am a lousy preacher, then, I need to make adjustments. If the person makes the claim out of bitterness or jealousy, we don't need to have the same response. Their assessment can also be the claims of a well-intentioned person that does not know any better. Let us consider several options as why I could become overly reactive to this example. First, I may truly believe that I am incompetent because I was told many years ago that God had not called me into the ministry. Second, I could feel incompetent because I am not fully trained to be in a pastoral position. Third, I might be fully trained, but I lack confidence in my speech. Fourth, I could be very sure of my speech and training, but I feel insecure about my leadership abilities because a previous church went through a painful division while I was their pastor, etc. The possibilities are endless.

It is not always possible to determine the different types of circumstances that can produce fear on a particular person. Therefore, people should not try to overcome their fears without first identifying their source. Rather, they should identify their reactive responses first, and then as they find a way to associate the fears to pasts experiences, they can find a more proactive response to their fears. A person does not have to stop being fearful of wild animals to live a healthy life. On the contrary, the fear of wild animals could be a very healthy approach to living. For instance, I suggest that being afraid of poisonous snakes is a healthy fear.

Eventually, people need to get to the point where they can make an association between their reactive behaviors and their spiritual injuries. When we can find a direct correlation between our defensiveness and a possible painful event in our past, we could begin the process to replace the lie created by the injury with the truth that I was created in God's image. Anything that distracts or corrupts God's image in us is a deceptive lie that must be uprooted.

The apostle Paul encouraged the Roman believers to "be transformed by the renewing of their minds" (Rom. 12:2). The mind needs to be transformed from the rebellious thinking against God, which is the result of our sinful condition that confines us to a temporal and fleshly thinking, to a new perspective in which we begin to think from an eternal and spiritual perspective. Paul desired that we develop a transformed mind. In order to make that possible, we need to renew our minds. And the only spiritual way to renew the mind is to recognize the lies we have believed all our lives and replaced them with the truth of God's word. In other words, there is only one way to uproot the lies that have enslaved us, and that is with the truth of God. Allow me to share a transformational principle: The only way to transform a mind is to replace the lies we have come to believe as a result of past irreconcilable contradictions with the truth of God's word about God and about the human condition.

The presence of blind spots is an indication that the spiritual injury has reached its final stage. It is necessary to state here that there is no set timeline to go from the catastrophic event to the blind spots. For some people, the movement could be very quickly. For others, it could take years before the symptoms that identify the presence of a blind spot become clear. But one thing is certain, the catastrophic event's final stage is the blind spot. Once a blind spot has been developed, it's there to stay. It's like the blind spot in a car, it's not going anywhere. The good news is that while, like in a car, the blind spots cannot be eliminated, they can be neutralized.

Blind spots do not produce pain or feelings of any kind. They are cognitive gaps in a person's ability to perceive the world around them. They block the person from preventing instinctive reactions to particular events. As soon as we become aware that certain attitudes and actions produce the same response, we can begin the process of accepting that a blind spot is present. Unless people are aware of the types of situations that make them reactive or defensive, they are susceptible to manipulation by people that know how to "push their buttons." Blind spots are similar to a sore on the skin that does not hurt but which makes us defensive and reactive to any suspicion that the sore might be touched. Obviously, the sore on the skin is not hidden, while the blind spot cannot be seen until the individuals have connected their reactivity and defensiveness to a specific spiritual injury. Whenever a situation brings back memories of the pain caused by a spiritual injury, there is going to be an instinctive reaction. Even when people are unaware of the emotional connection between their blind spots and their spiritual injuries, their reactiveness should be taken as a signpost that the connection exists. The recognition of the instinctive behavior helps people to accept the presence of a blind spot, which in turn helps them accept their brokenness.

Accepting that our hearts have been broken is a non-negotiable aspect of the healing process. I know many people would like to present a front of absolute strength and health. This attitude is counterproductive, especially if the person is already engaged in self-destructive behaviors. Our desire is to move people from injury to health before they hit rock bottom. However, if they have hit rock bottom, then, this book is essential to escape the trap. When an event or situation, unrelated to the original trauma, awakens memories of the contradiction, this allows people to make the connection between their reactivity and their injury much faster. This realization could facilitate the discussion that will expose the blind spot. This is the essential step in becoming proactive to neutralize the blind spot.

Allow me to share another personal example. There was a time in which whenever I would go to a restaurant, I would become quite agitated if the waitress did not attend us in a timely manner. My agitation could turn into anger if people whom I knew arrived after us were served before us. I know many people have similar reactions, but I had to find out why this situation could create that much anxiety and anger in me. After a few incidents, it became clear that my behavior was irrational because, in the scheme of things, being served five or ten minutes late was an insignificant event.

Eventually, I was able to accept the possibility that I had an irreconcilable contradiction traceable to my abandonment as a child. My father left when I was two, and my mother left when I was four. I never blamed them for their decisions. They were young and inexperienced. They made the best decision they could with their circumstances. As an adult, I have maintained a very cordial and friendly relationship with both of them. However, the fact that I never blamed them does not negate the possibility that growing up without my biological parents may have become an irreconcilable contradiction that turned into the spiritual injury of abandonment. This injury eventually turned into the blind spot that associates a perceived neglect of service by a waitress to my parents' abandonment. As a direct result of my parents' abandonment in childhood, I experience most events through the abandonment filter. Generally, I do not experience many other situations that produce the same type of reactivity in my heart. This fact allowed me to pinpoint the source to the abandonment I felt growing up.

Recognizing my behavior was not difficult. The difficult part was making a connection to a spiritual injury I did not even know existed. I knew I could become uncomfortable and reactive when the waitress was not prompt. I also knew I did not like my negative reactions, but they always appeared to catch me off guard. Something had to change. Since I was not fully aware of the intensity of my own reactions, there was not much I could do to change them. My overreactions to the *restaurant neglect syndrome* (not a real illness) went on for years until a friend pointed out the incongruence between the behavior and my character. This is the nature of blind spots. They produce instinctive, and on occasion violent, reactions to otherwise insignificant events. The goal is to become aware of our reactions to become proactive against the reactivity caused by the blind spots. Let me talk a little about physical blindness as a metaphor for the spiritual blind spots.

The apostle John wrote extensively about both types of blindness. John spoke about darkness, night, blindness, lack of understanding, and unbelief as forms of spiritual blindness. I suggest to you that he was not merely describing people's feelings and choices. I believe the biblical discussion about blindness is a reference to a hardening of people's hearts to the point that they are unable or unwilling to believe God's revealed truth, especially in the person of Jesus Christ. Spiritual blindness is a deep-seated condition of the heart that prevents people to come to a full knowledge of God.

Created as Spiritual Beings

As we have already discussed that the term spiritual injury assumes that we are more than just flesh and bones. Our spirituality is the expression of God's invisible image within us. It is clearly different from our physical experience of life. Human life is incomprehensible without an understanding of how God's personality traits define us, specifically, in relationship to God's character. Most people are aware of their dual formation; they are physical creatures with a spiritual component. However, most people do not grasp fully the significance of the spiritual aspect that manages their emotions, their ability to process information, and their knowledge of good and evil. Some have argued that true science (here you can read: atheistic or Darwinian evolution) requires that we discard anything spiritual.

The proponents of this atheistic science live with an inherent hypocrisy.[10] Barash defined their hypocrisy this way. These scientists believe in absolute biological determinism, but they live as "if freewill reign supreme."[11] Their rejection of moral freedom is the rejection of the very thing that allows them to make their arguments. But, they

---

[10]   Barash.

[11]   Ibid.

must reject moral freedom because this is a distinctively Christian concept, and Christianity is the very thing they want to destroy. This attitude is the most persistent and rigid blind spot for postmodern society. They simply don't have solutions to the broken heart because they reject the very idea that people may even have a spiritual soul. These people hold these ideas even though addictions are everywhere in society. This is the reason that, an honest atheist like Barash, recognizes the hypocrisy of the scientific community.

Therefore, the deniers of our spiritual character qualities don't even realize they are also rejecting our very consciousness of the world around us. Our consciousness cannot be explained with atoms and molecules. It is a component of our existence that resides in a different realm from matter and the physical world. We are aware of our existence as well as the existence of the other. If our lives were defined through simple biological processes, we would not have any feelings associated with non-material character traits. But that is not the case.

For example, some of our non-physical qualities that define, and that are intrinsic to our humanity include, guilt, shame, the need to take responsibility for our actions, and a sense of accountability to others and to God. These are undeniable aspects of the human experience that cannot be explained through our senses. But they are as real to us as our own skin. This is the reason I say that we need to come to terms with the spiritual aspect of our human existence. If we want to build a bridge that allows people to cross from their addictions and dysfunctional self-destructive behaviors to spiritual health, we must recognize our own spirituality. If we accept the concept that we are spiritual beings, as we have discussed, then, we can proceed to discuss how we struggle with the irreconcilable contradictions created by spiritual injuries. Let us take a look at Jesus's teaching about spiritual blindness through the healing of the man born blind.

Healing Blind Hearts

In the book of John, we find one of the most powerful stories in the Bible. Jesus met a man that had been born blind (Jn. 9:1-41). The religious tradition of the time would judge the blind man's condition solely from a legalistic perspective. They understood the man's blindness as a direct consequence of sin. It was not a surprise that the disciples had assumed some sin in the man's life when they asked Jesus, "Who sinned, this man or his parents, that he was born blind?" (Jn. 9:2). Jesus answered that neither, the man nor his parents had sinned. Jesus, then, healed the man and sent him home with sight.

Jesus's answer did not fit the conventional wisdom of the day. Do not miss his point here. Jesus had not merely healed the blind man. Since the man was born blind, Jesus had to recreate the entire optic system in the man's eyes, and he had to open the brain's ability to read light as it entered through the now restored vision for the first time in his life. Jesus said, "The eye is the lamp of the body. If your eye is healthy, your whole body will be full of light. But if your eye is bad, your whole body will be full of darkness. If then the light within you is darkness, how great is the darkness!" (Matt. 6:22-23) Jesus's message is quite compelling. If people only have partial visions their whole existence is in darkness, but imagine the deep their blindness would be, if their spiritual life did not even have the partial light of a bad eye.

The real controversy began after Jesus had performed the miracle and the people recognized that the blind man had received his sight. The Pharisees started an investigation of the event, but not because they were unaware of the claims. They needed to discredit the miracle to refute Jesus's authority. They could not allow people to believe that the Messiah was among them.

Jesus took the opportunity of this controversy to interject the teaching on the dangers of spiritual blindness. The real issue here was that the religious leaders had designed a worldview that excluded faith in God's promised Messiah as a suffering servant. As a result, they had developed spiritual blind spots that prevented them from recognizing Jesus as God's Son. Their worldview was an internal contradiction between what they believed to be true (the Messiah has not come) and what was actually true (the Messiah was among them in the person of Jesus). As we have already discussed, blind spots are the result of spiritual injuries that make the person instinctively reactive and defensive against anything that threatens their established reality. The religious leaders of Jesus's day had a blind spot that had shut off the reality of the spiritual world in which God resides as an explanation for their religious existence. John declared that Jesus was the Light of the world (Jn. 1:4-9). Jesus's assumption was that anyone with healthy spiritual eyes should have been able to see him for who he was. The purpose of the Light was to bring illumination into the darkness of men's hearts. There is one condition. The spiritual optic nerve must be in working order. The deepest darkness belongs to the man who, in his own righteousness and pride, rejects the light (the truth) entering in his soul.

Jesus, as the Light of God's Word, came to restore the sight for men and women. This was Jesus's point about the man born blind. We are blind to the things of the Spirit by virtue of our sinful condition—just as the man born blind had suffered the ravages of sin on his physical body. And just like the man born blind, we need Jesus's intervention to have our spiritual sight restored.

Darkness, as a condition, is not exclusive to the lost. Many saved people have areas in their lives that are darkened by sin or by brokenness. This is not to say that they are not saved or that they are outside fellowship with God. These dark areas (blind spots) require illumination. This is the case of people having the ability to see, but having "a log" blocking the light (Matt. 7:4). People must remove the obstacle so that they can assimilate Jesus's light. These dark pockets are spiritually or emotionally sensitive areas in the soul that prevent others from having access to them. Some people even try to keep God out. This is not to say that God does not know how these dark areas affect a person. On the contrary, we know that God knows, but we are still unable to overcome the darkness (guilt and shame) to face God. We keep our fears hidden inside hoping that no one, including God, will notice. This is self-deceptive and wishful thinking.

Our desire to hide from God was inherited from Adam and Eve. Sin became their blind spot and our inheritance. Their response to their shame lingers to this day. We have convinced ourselves that not even God should have access to our shame. As far as we are concerned, God has become too intrusive. The contrast between human sin and God's holiness is an obstacle that makes it difficult for us to understand God as good, caring, and gracious. This is one of the reasons many people reject God today. How can a good God, they ask, allow so much suffering in the world? Many people perceive him as judgmental, ruthless, and uncaring. So, we ask the question, does God really care about our suffering? All of us have secrets, and we do not want anyone to know them, including God. Those secrets are not to be shared. They hurt too much. In the process of hiding our shame, we condemn ourselves to endless suffering and pain behind the shadows. We have not discovered that our hiddenness strengthens the sins that caused the shame and the broken fellowship with God.

The Pharisees were the spiritual guides of Jesus's day, but they had been blinded by their pride. They lacked the necessary spiritual insight to recognize Jesus's light. If anyone should have been able to recognize God's message, it should have been the Pharisees. The opposite was true. Their religion, the instrument that should have been their salvation, had created the darkened areas in their souls. Their spiritual optic nerve (the possibility of faith) was damaged. The Pharisees were unable to recognize God's message being preached by and through Jesus. The blind spot created by their religious legalism would not allow them to believe.

The Pharisees' blindness to spiritual truth was the result of a prideful devotion to the Law. They had reinterpreted God's truth to look more like their own cultural preferences. This is the reason Paul asserted that the Law is spiritual, and it was given with the purpose to guide the conscience. However, the religious leaders had reinterpreted the Law mostly as a set of rules to regulate conduct. This contradiction became a spiritual injury for the Pharisees, which eventually became their blind spot. When Jesus came, they could not see him because his behavior did not conform to their interpretation of the Law.

The Law did not provide a way out of the sinful condition. As a result of that failure of the Law, the Pharisees projected their spiritual contradiction onto the people. They misunderstood and misapplied the Law, and the people were paying for their blindness. This is the reason Jesus said: "If the blind leads the blind, both will fall into the pit" (Matt. 15:14). Additionally, Jesus made the following clarifications about the Law (Matt. 5:17-48). He used the phrase "you have heard...but I tell you" six times in this passage. The Pharisees had misunderstood the Law as a series of *do's and don'ts*. Jesus, on the other hand, understood the Law, both as a guide to discern people's motives and as God's prescription for godly living. The Pharisees' pride prevented them from examining their own attitudes and motives. They were convinced they had the truth, but they were the blind guiding the blind.

As stated earlier, blind spots make people susceptible to believe in lies, or to hide from the truth. If they knew that only the truth can overcome lies, they could have seen the light that Jesus brought to the world. The lies could be philosophical, political, relational, or historical. Jesus's presence represented a contradiction for them because he brought the truth with him. For the rest of Jesus's ministry, the Pharisees were mostly preoccupied with judging his behavior to discredit his message. For them to accept Jesus's message would have been to acknowledge that they had believed lies.

The healing of the man born blind was the climax of the confrontation between Jesus and the Pharisees. This event was even more critical than the raising of Lazarus. It was in this chapter that Jesus exposed the religious leaders as the blind guiding of the blind. They had instinctive and predictable negative reactions to spiritual truth. Jesus knew of their blindness and exposed them at every term, but they refused to change. Their reactions were predictable because they behaved like men living in darkness. This is the reason Jesus said to them: "If you were Abraham's children, you would be doing the works Abraham did, but now you seek to kill me, a man who has told you the truth that I heard from God. This is not what Abraham did" (Jn. 8:39-40). In other words, they believed the lies the devil was propagating instead of the truth Jesus was teaching them.

The religious leaders were sure that they were following the Law of Moses. Listen to their words. "Then they hurled insults at him and said, 'You are this fellow's disciple!' We are disciples of Moses! We know that God spoke to Moses, but as for this fellow, we don't even know where he comes from'" (Jn. 9:28-29). They had forgotten that it was not Moses's Law. It was God's Law. They were totally committed to the Law and to Moses, but as a result of their blind commitment they had failed to see that Moses had spoken about the Christ.

Physically blind people do not have to be told they are blind. They are fully aware of their condition. The same is not true for spiritually blinded people. The spiritually blind are not aware of their blindness, or of the causes for their blindness. They have come to believe that the world is in reality exactly as they experience it. Spiritually blinded people see the rest of the world as being wrong for not believing as they do. As stated earlier, there is one remedy for spiritual blindness—they need an encounter with an objective truth outside of themselves. Only God can provide this objective truth. As long as spiritually blinded people believe that they possess the truth independently of God, they will remain blind. John, in his customary masterful way, used physical language to describe this spiritual truth. When the Pharisees asked the question, "Are we blind too?" Jesus replied: "If you were blind, you would not be guilty of sin; but now that you claim you can see, your guilt remains" (Jn. 9:40-41).

Jesus's point was that blind people know they are blind and are willing to accept that fact without much argument. But spiritually blind people refuse to accept the error of their ways, even at the expense of the truth. The spiritually blind can see by accepting the light of the truth. But when the spiritually blind reject the truth, their sin (their blindness) will remain. That's the point of spiritual blindness—men refuse to accept God's truth. It is not that they cannot accept the truth. It is that they refuse to accept it. Jesus stated that God had tried to bring Jerusalem to repentance, but they "were not willing" (Lk. 13:34).

There are two basic reasons people are not willing to accept the truth. First, pride blinds people to their own needs. The proud person has difficulties accepting their sins, their errors, and their need to change their ways. The second reason is love for the world. Jesus stated that people reject the light because they love darkness more than the light.

There are three other types of spiritual blindness mentioned in Scripture. First is the spiritual blindness produced by an unyielding legalistic belief system. Legalistic systems are very rigid regarding external practices. The most important aspect of religious legalism is conformity to codes of conduct. People participating in legalistic systems develop a spirit of superiority. They feel better than others because they are willing to make the necessary sacrifices to live according to the dictates of their moral codes. These systems have two fundamental flaws: they have the tendency to claim exclusive access to the truth, and they have the need to eliminate competition from the arena of ideas. Legalistic belief systems produce a self-centered pride that necessarily looks at those outside the system as inferior, or as being downright evil.

When these types of systems are in full force, they become too hardened to be useful. This was the blindness that afflicted the Pharisees—they could not connect with the people while claiming to be their guides. The religious leaders of Jesus's day were committed to the Law and their spiritual optic nerve was damaged by their reluctance to receive new information. The Pharisees did not want to hear anything that may have shed light on their spiritual condition. After all, they had dedicated their entire lives to upholding the Law as they understood it—it was too late for them to change. The light of God's Word could not penetrate a damaged spiritual optic nerve. They had all the information they needed, but they chose not to act upon it.

Then, we have the blindness produced by lack of information. This is the person who does not see, but it is not because any damage to the spiritual optic nerve. Rather, this person cannot see because they do not know what they are looking for. They are ready to respond to the truth, but the truth has not reached them yet. Once the light (truth) shines on them, people in this category have no problem accepting its blessings. Their spiritual optic nerve has not been hardened with an unyielding belief system, and they are open to receive new revelation.

For example, the man that was born blind was available and open to receive new information, but he had not been properly instructed. Soon after he had received his sight, Jesus revealed himself to the man, and he "worshiped [Jesus]" (Jn. 9:38). He was ready and available to believe and worship, which is the basic understanding of receiving spiritual sight. The prophet declared: "My people perish for lack of knowledge" (Hos. 4:6). This phrase has at least two possible meanings: (1) people have not received knowledge or (2) people have refused to act upon the knowledge they already have. Regardless of the reasons for our lack of knowledge, the result is the same—people perish without it.

The third form of spiritual blindness is the one created by spiritual injuries. Negative experiences can prevent us from recognizing some aspects of God's truths. In these cases, people do not suffer from the spiritual blindness of the Pharisees, or of the neo-atheist. Often people in this category are believers that have difficulties grasping the fullness of God's grace. For example, Solomon, who was the wisest man that ever lived, had this type of spiritual blindness. He spoke extensively and eloquently about the dangers of multiple marital entanglements. And yet he almost never lived according to his own advice by keeping more than one thousand women in his household. How can the wisest man that ever lived be so susceptible to making the exact mistake he warned others against?

I suggest to you that Solomon had suffered a spiritual injury that turned into a blind spot in relationships. At some point in his life, he must have found out that his mother Bathsheba had an affair with his father David. He also must have found out that David had his mother's husband killed. These must have been a shameful series of events for Solomon. Imagine Solomon as a young man living in the king's palace listening to the whispers behind the curtains about David and his mother. This is the kind of story that leaves permanent spiritual marks in a person. While the Bible does not specifically identify this type of spiritual blindness, there are multiple examples contained in Scripture that can only be explained from the perspective of a spiritual injury.

Spiritual blindness is the condition that prevents people from appreciating the spiritual dimension of the world around them. In matters of salvation, spiritual blindness mostly refers to unbelievers. However, Christians can also experience the spiritual blindness the Bible identifies as immaturity. Being an immature Christian means that believers have not attained the necessary wisdom to comprehend and apply eternal truths to their daily living. They believe the truth as revealed in Scripture, but they are not able to grasp the full meaning of how the truth applies practically to their lives. Their inability to grasp eternal truths translates into a worldly mindset for the Christian, mostly because immature Christians continue explaining their relationship with God from a worldly perspective. The church has the task of helping the new Christian move past this stage of their spiritual development through an intentional discipleship process. This problem is so prevalent that, according to Paul, unbelievers and baby Christians are indistinguishable in their conduct. The difference lies in that the baby Christian has embarked in the journey to "be conformed to the image of Christ" while the unbeliever remains unredeemed by refusing to accept the truth of God's revelation in Christ (1 Cor. 3:1-4; Rom. 8:29).

A blind spot is different from other forms of blindness in that it is limited in scope. Spiritual blindness leads to eternal death as a result of unbelief. Blind spots, on the other hand, are dangerous and could also be deadly. They block a limited area of the individuals' spiritual awareness, but they do not lead to eternal death. Blind spots are common even for the saved person. Their common occurrence is due to their connection to spiritual injuries, which are a routine aspect of the human experience. However, since individuals have different coping skills, the resulting blind spot does not have the same effect on everyone. The Church could play a major role for Christians to overcome the compulsive nature of blind spots through the exercise of spiritual disciplines, which include truth telling and transparency. Through a discipleship process based on God's character that leads to a deeper insight into who we are, the Christian grows in the knowledge of God's eternal truths. This is the maturing process that every Christian embarks upon receiving Christ as Savior.

The Nature of Blindness

Physical blindness occurs when the *optic nerve* is either damaged or paralyzed, preventing light from entering into the brain.[12] Without light entering the brain, there is no information for the brain to

---

[12]   NOTE: I am using the phrase optic nerve as a metaphor and not as a medical or scientific term.

process to make sense of the external world. Without light, we cannot appreciate the world around us.

Conversely, spiritual blindness occurs when the *spiritual optic nerve* does not allow the light of God's Word to enter a man's heart. The Bible uses the phrase that Pharaoh "hardened his heart" as a metaphor for spiritual blindness (Ex. 7:13). Paul's prayer for the Ephesian church included the phrase that, "having the eyes of your hearts enlightened, that you may know what is the hope to which he has called you" (Eph. 1:18). Paul understood that without the light of God's Word we would lack an essential element to replace the lies we have believed all our lives with the truth of God's character. Paul's message was that we need to encourage people to become receptive to the proclamation of the truth of the gospel message. To see the truth, we need the Creator's perspective.

The Nature of Blind Spots

A car's blind spot, as I mentioned earlier, is an area on the vehicle that is not visible to the driver. The rearview mirrors are not enough to overcome a vehicle's blind spots. The fact that drivers may not be aware of the blind areas around their cars does not negate their existence. Drivers can overcome their vehicles' blind spots when they know where they are and can take preventive action to neutralize their danger. Inexperienced drivers, on the highway for the first time, may not be aware of the blind spots on both sides of their vehicles. Their inability to see approaching vehicles on their right or left sides does not protect them from a possible accident. The driver does not want to have an accident. However, if drivers do not know how to neutralize their cars' blind spots, they are closer to an accident than they are aware. If the driver changes lanes without recognizing the presence of the blind spots, he could drift into incoming traffic unintentionally. Their move to the right or left lane was innocent enough, but since inexperienced drivers might be ignorant regarding their cars' blind spots, they may not have known their own car was hiding upcoming traffic from view.

These drivers could make all kinds of excuses to the police for the reasons they got into the accident. "I did not see the car." "I did not intend to get in an accident." "This is my father's car." "This is my first time on the highway." The excuses do not matter. The blind spots do not care about your feelings. A blind spot just is. People either know they are there and address them, as best they can, or they will drift into reoccurring accidents. Every driver should know that cars have blind spots and should take precautionary measures accordingly. As we have already seen, blind spots are not limited to cars. Every person on this planet has them, even if most people are not aware of their existence. And yet blind spots are as real as our ability to think or breathe.

Bill McCartney once wrote, "Some of us just don't want to see certain things."[13] This was the problem with the Pharisees during Jesus's time. They could not bring themselves to believe that their Messiah had come and nobody had told them. The contradiction between their self-importance (what they believed about themselves) and the fact that they were not informed about the coming Messiah (the reality around them) had blinded them to Jesus. They were accustomed to leading every religious event. But the Messiah had come, and nobody informed them of his appearing. Allow me to share three attitudes regarding blind spots.

The first attitude people refuse to accept is the possibility they may, in fact, have a blind spot. Isaiah described the Pharisees' attitude when he said: "Lead out those who have eyes but are blind, who have ears but are deaf" (Isa. 43:8). The blindness of the religious leaders of Jesus's time was greater than the blindness of the man born blind. At least the man born blind was able to recognize Jesus as soon as he saw him, while the Pharisees could not see him even after he had performed many miracles among them. The man born blind received physical as well as spiritual sight. In contrast, the religious leaders, who claimed to see, suffered the worst kind of blindness—a blindness of the spirit that kept them ignorant of God's true revelation in Christ. Healing a blind man is not a big deal to God. After all,

---

[13] Bill McCartney. Blind Spots: What You Don't See Might be Keeping Your Church From Greatness. (Promise Keepers, 2003), p. 9

he created the eye. But opening the spiritual eyes of a person is a much more complicated transaction. God has chosen not to violate our moral freedom even if it means that we will continue to walk in darkness. God's light shines, but "men love darkness more than the light because their deeds were evil" (Jn. 3:19). God pleads with us to let his light in, but God's light cannot be effective in sinners' souls until they choose to accept it.

The Pharisees asked Jesus the following question. "What? Are we blind too?" (Jn. 9:40) The question did not need an answer because the answer was implied with the question. Yes, you are blind. If they were not blind, they would have been able to recognize Jesus. The Pharisees sat at Moses's seat, but could not recognize the One Moses spoke about. Jesus's answer was brilliant. He said, "If you were blind, you would not be guilty of sin; but now that you claim you can see, your guilt remains" (Jn. 9:41). Jesus described the Pharisees' blindness as a willful and stubborn decision to refuse to see what should have been readily apparent to them. The Pharisees' ignorance and self-deception were exposed when Jesus gave sight to the blind man. They could also have received God's light through Jesus if they had acknowledged who he was. But instead they claimed to see (to have understanding), and their confession was their judgment. If they were truly ignorant, Jesus may have considered them innocent. In the same way that Jesus offered forgiveness to the blind man, the Pharisees could have asked and received the same forgiveness.

Jesus would have extended his grace to the Pharisees, as he did to many of them individually, but their pride did not allow them to accept Jesus's testimony. Instead of moving to faith after Jesus opened the eyes of the blind man, they moved to blasphemy. The Pharisees represent the person that refuses to come to grips with his own personal blindness (prejudices). They simply refused to see. Or said in another way, the Pharisees are the kind of people who know their cars have blind spots that can cause an accident, but refuse to take action. They were blind guides of the blind (or, they were the ignorant guiding the ignorant). Their pride and stubbornness drove them and their followers into the pit.

The second attitude is feeling powerless to make the necessary adjustments. The apostle Paul described the sinful condition as an enemy living within us. His desire was to do what was right, but there was a power inside him that pushed him to sin (Rom. 7). He was blinded by his sinful desires. The flesh would cause him to stumble when he least expected it. Paul understood the power the flesh had over him. But in spite of the fact that he recognized the sinfulness within, he lacked the power to overcome its influence on his own. He needed the Holy Spirit action in his life. This is not to say the apostle was making excuses for evil behavior. On the contrary, Paul was committed to doing God's will, but he could not escape the contradiction in his spirit between his desire to do good and his temptation to sin. This is how he describes his struggle:

> We know that the law is spiritual; but I am unspiritual, sold as a slave to sin. I do not understand what I do. For what I want to do I do not do, but what I hate I do. And if I do what I do not want to do, I agree that the law is good. As it is, it is no longer I myself who do it, but it is sin living in me. I know that nothing good lives in me, that is, in my sinful nature. For I have the desire to do what is good, but I cannot carry it out. For what I do is not the good I want to do; no, the evil I do not want to do—this I keep on doing. Now if I do what I do not want to do, it is no longer I who do it, but it is sin living in me that does it (Rom. 7:14-20).

Paul's point is that our sinful condition is responsible for our instinctive impulses to sinful attitudes and behaviors. The sinful nature is a metaphor to describe our innate bent towards rebellion against God. This bent toward evil is so ingrained in our subconscious that we are not even aware when the flesh is controlling our thinking. In other words, our sinful nature itself is a blind spot that prevents us from living a life pleasing to God. We really cannot help ourselves unless we surrender to the Holy Spirit's work in our lives. We were created to be good, but sin reprogrammed us to do evil. A blind spot created by a spiritual injury has the same effect in our souls as the sinful condition—they function like vacuums in our consciences that prevent us from realizing our own instinctive reactivity and defensiveness to people and events.

The third attitude is that people are not even aware they have blind spots. This is the most prevalent and dangerous attitude because people go from temptation to temptation without realizing the conditions that make them vulnerable. The suggestion that people are not aware of their own blind spots is not an exaggeration. Some of these blind spots are the result of superficial injuries and thus, they do not have crippling effects on our relationships. That is, while blind spots created by superficial injuries may have contributed to shaping our character they have not made us instinctively reactive to circumstances.

However, the blind spots created by a catastrophic spiritual injury have a controlling effect in people's ability to interact with their environment. The instinctive reactivity is the normal response to anything that may remind people of the original spiritual injury. This is the reason we want to focus our attention in the process to identify blind spots. If we are able to identify the reactivity or defensiveness, then we have an opportunity to identify the catastrophic spiritual injury. This process is essential to develop proactive responses to the "knowledge vacuum" we have called blind spots.

Over the next few paragraphs I will share the three emotional symptoms people exhibit that indicate the presence of a blind spot, which in turn means that a spiritual injury has occurred.

Identifying Blind Spots

Most people do not have difficulties recognizing critical events in their lives. People can remember when they were lost in the woods as teenagers and a feeling of panic that overtook them, or when they broke a leg falling from a horse, etc. The problem most people have is identifying whether a particular event left a permanent spiritual scar (a mark) in their character.

Allow me to illustrate. Growing up in Puerto Rico, during the summers we would go to the rivers to swim. We would spend hours playing, jumping from rocks into the rivers, and swimming. I was not an expert swimmer, but I held my own. I remember one particular day when we were playing a game and two friends were holding my legs up in the water. For a while, I was able to keep myself afloat by balancing myself with my arms, but as the game continued, my arms became tired. Twice I went under water. My friends thought this was funny, but I began to feel a sense of panic and started kicking as hard as I could to get myself free. Finally, they released me, and I swam to the side of the river. I was relieved, but I was also very frustrated and angry.

That event is still very vivid in my memory. I have never had any problems going to swimming pools, rivers, or the beach. I can still swim without any particular fears. For years, I could not identify any visible or hidden issues associated with that particular event. Then I became a father. One day we took the children to the pool for a day of fun, and while the children were jumping in the water and having fun, I found myself on the side of the pool in a near state of panic. I could not get in the water because I wanted to be able to respond just in case one of the kids got in trouble. All of a sudden, I realized that my panic at seeing my children around the water was directly connected to my experience as a thirteen-year-old in a small river in Puerto Rico.

This is the problem that most people face. They, like me, can identify the traumatic events in their lives. However, most people cannot connect the dots of present behavior to a particular event in the past. This is what we know: every event or experience has a cumulative effect in our character. We become what we have experienced throughout our lives. Therefore, if we are going to know whether an event has turned into a spiritual injury, we need to identify the behaviors and reactions that point people back to the original event.

First: Instinctive Reactivity

Spiritual injuries produce erratic relationships because of the damage they do to the intimacy mechanism. A damaged intimacy mechanism manifests itself mostly in the form of false shame. False shame is not merely negative feelings. When false shame is the result of a spiritual injury that damages the intimacy mechanism, it becomes an instinctive expression of the self. People feel real shame for personal sins, potentially leading to repentance and wholeness. False shame never produces sincere repentance and reconciliation, because it is the result of the internalization of the behavior of the perpetrator. Shame is internalized when injured individuals blame themselves for their victimization. An example of this could be when children suffer from sexual abuse. If the abuser is successful in passing the blame to them, the victims have the tendency to assume responsibility for their victimization. This vicious manipulation shifts the shame from the victimizer to the victim. An example of this false shame is the Stockholm Syndrome.

The Stockholm Syndrome is the psychological term that defines the cases in which the victim assumes the shame of the victimizer. The Stockholm Syndrome describes the behavior of kidnap victims who, over time, become sympathetic to their captors. The name derives from a 1973 hostage incident in Stockholm, Sweden.[14] At the end of six days of captivity in a bank, several kidnap victims actually resisted rescue attempts, and afterwards refused to testify against their captors. When the victim of abuse internalizes the victimizer's shame, they have developed a false sense of shame.

False shame traps individuals into believing they have the need to repent for their role in the event that caused their injury. In order for people to overcome their shame, they must be able to identify the violence of their perpetrators. However, once people have identified with the perpetrator's violence, overcoming their false shame is a very difficult task indeed. People cannot repent or reconcile based on someone else's actions. This would be analogous to asking a victim of rape to repent for her role in the rape. This request would victimize the woman twice. First, she was the victim of the rape. Then, she is victimized by the demand to repent for a sin she did not commit. The rape victim, like the individual who was abused as a child, has not done anything for which to repent.

---

[14]   Stockholm Syndrome.

Second: Impulsive Negativity

A reaction is a negative emotional response to a person or a situation that creates discomfort or fear. These negative reactions tend to be instinctive in nature. They suggest a subconscious need to avoid an unidentified spiritual contradiction. On occasions people know why they are having these reactions, but they cannot stop themselves. Until people become fully aware of the events or people that trigger their reactions, they will struggle with their negative reactivity.

The goal is to become aware of how the original brokenness can condition people's perception of the reality around them. When people come to terms with the spiritual injury that altered their character, they can plan a proactive response to the situations that resemble their spiritual injury. This would allow the person to turn his defensiveness into a healthier proactive response to situations and people. As we have already discussed, most people can identify the injury responsible for their pain. The problem is in making the connection between the spiritual injury and its corresponding blind spot. This is the area in which the instinctive reactivity plays its biggest role. When people have reactive reactions, chances are, they know the event that produces these reactions. Thus, in spite of the difficulty people have in making the connection between the source of their pain and their blind spots, I suggest we can begin with making the connection between our reactivity to people and events and the present cause that provoked it. It is important to note that these negative reactions are defense mechanisms to elude the discomfort caused by the original spiritual injury as the person experience it in the present events. I have discovered that any situation, or words, that may bring back the memory of the original injury produces these unconscious reactions and these reactions are indicators of the presence of a blind spot, which in turn is the result of the irreconcilable contradiction that was produced by a traumatic event.

These reactions are instinctive because people do not have to *think* about them before responding. In many instances, people are not able to override or prevent these reactions because by the time they realize what is happening they have already taken the action. One of the dangers of our reactions is that we are not fully aware how they impact other people. Probably all of us have heard sarcastic comments directed at us and before we had assimilated what the person was trying to say, we have responded with another sarcastic remark. This is the natural response to sarcasm in everyday conversations. Have you ever regretted a response because it might have gone over the top, or it may have created the wrong impression of what you were trying to say? Normally, regrets come after we have put our foot in our mouths, which is a daily occurrence for some people. These common interactions lead me to ask the question: what steps can we take to avoid this emotional roller coaster of impulsive reactivity?

We can summarize our reactivity to uncomfortable situations as instinctive, negative, unconscious, and with a defensive attitude. Allow me to suggest three practical approaches to manage our negative reactions.

First, people need to make a situation analysis after each reactive response. Whenever a situation leaves a bad taste in our mouths, we need to go back to the event and ask a series of questions: "What happened?" There are several things we need to know. What was said or done and what was my response? Who said it and how did I understand it? What was the context, and was I aware of the context and the intent of the statement or of the event? What was the tone of voice and why did impact me in such a negative way? What triggered my reaction? Did I feel threatened or disrespected?

Whatever answer we come up with, the response needs to be expressed in feelings language. For example, instead of saying, "The waitress is an idiot"; I could say, "When the waitress did not serve me in a timely manner I felt disrespected." The first response is a personal judgment against the waitress, who probably is not at fault. The second response is my reflection regarding an event that did not match my expectations for that situation. It is also a more appropriate response because instead of reacting to the perceived neglect from the waitress, I am reflecting on my own attitude. This is a more appropriate and fair statement regarding the situation because since I don't have all the information that prevented the waitress from serving me in the appropriate term, it is an unfair accusation that the waitress is an idiot for something she did not control. Besides, I have no empirical evidence to the waitress's intelligence level. For all I know, she could be the number one graduate of her college class. I need to describe my inner turmoil and not what I perceive as the waitress's carelessness.

Generally speaking, the initial feeling describing the situation is not the bottom line issue, especially if people's initial response is anger. Expressing our reactions from a feelings perspective gives us insight into what is going on in our subconscious. Using feelings to evaluate the event gives proper context to the problem at hand because our reactions were emotionally based. Thus, expressing our responses in feelings language better describes the emotional triggers that produced the reaction. Once people accept the emotional aspect of their reactivity, they would be better prepared to define their situation, which gives them greater insight into the effect of the spiritual injury.

Men will struggle in this area more than women, but not for the reasons most people think. Men are as able as women to express their feelings. However, men are more reluctant to do so because of a cultural bias that associates the expression of feelings with feminine qualities. Additionally, since men's starting point for relationships is logic, their first impulse is rarely expressed through feelings. That is, men can express their feelings, but only after they have seen the logic of the event. Therefore, when dealing with men we have to allow more time for them to find the necessary composure to express the feelings honestly. Otherwise, some men would mimic expressing feelings without being fully transparent. Many men have to work through the perceived contradiction that feelings are signs of weakness before they can make a genuine feeling statement. In some instances, a subtle coaching might be necessary. Some men may express a strong reaction against making feelings statements because as a child they were told that boys could not cry or feel like girls. This lie has become seared into many men's sub-consciences and it has to be replaced with a more truthful statement about male feelings. Some men have actually stormed out of my office after making the statement that their feelings were irrelevant to the issue at hand.

Second, do not dismiss a friend's observations to your defensive reactions without first making a dispassionate evaluation of the validity of those observations. Many times, people get offended with a friend for pointing out their negative reactions or a defensive attitude over a situation. It is natural to be dismissive of a friend's comment in the heat of the moment. But after the emotions have cooled down and they are alone with their thoughts, they need to ask the question, "Why did Joe say I was defensive or reactive?" I will share two possible alternatives.

First, is that people need to be honest about evaluating their inner feelings. And they need to be honest with their own negative reaction to their friend's comments. Accepting input from our friends is essential if we are going to make healthy corrections to our reactivity. One problem still remains with this situation. When the trauma that caused the spiritual injury becomes a determining factor in our character, we may not be able to do the necessary self-assessment regarding our friend's input at the moment of the event. While a hidden blind spot could stop us from receiving feedback from a friend, we need to work diligently to identify the blind spots before they become a crippling handicap. Trusting a friend is a key aspect to overcome our fears because a friend can describe our reaction in a non-judgmental way. Additionally, we also need to have the courage to accept the truthfulness of his words.

Another suggestion is that people need to make adjustment to the expectations they bring to their daily interactions. Let me provide a simple definition. *Expectations are personal standards acquired over years of experiences that we project onto other people.* All of us have developed personal standards we abide by. These standards, while not always kept perfectly, give us confidence to respond to circumstances and people. There is one key element that could help us prevent projecting our standards onto others. We have to recognize that our personal standards are based on our personal experiences, developed over the course of years, and that others have not shared those experiences with us. Our home environment and our cultural experiences shaped our understanding of how the world functions. Even someone who grew up in the same neighborhood, or even in the same household, does not share the same experiences. There is at least one reason for this. Two people in the same context cannot respond to a shared event with the same emotional intensity. Personal experiences are unique to each individual because people are different. This is the reason that personal experiences have limited value as tools to establish societal or spiritual principles, and they should be understood as such.

For example: growing up I had a difficult time understanding God as a Father because my earthly father left us when I was about three-years-old. Our grandmother, who was a faithful Christian, introduced us to a father figure that served as a spiritual guide for me. He was the pastor of the church I grew up in. She also gave us the gift of faith through the example of a gentle pastor who played the father role for us. While I was able later in life to identify with God as a Father, as a teenager I was not able to relate with God as a Father. The image I used to relate to God was that of a Friend. It wasn't until I became a father myself that I was able to fully grasp the significance of God's role as a Father.

Most people with whom we interact do not necessarily share our standards because they have not shared our experiences. Personal and cultural standards are often intertwined, and on many occasions, they become indistinguishable. However, individuals within a society do not always conform to the accepted cultural expressions. For instance, the American culture places a high value on timeliness. This cultural standard is generally accepted as a good thing. But, does the fact that the American culture frowns on tardiness mean that Americans are never late? Of course not! The personal standard regarding timeliness is often not as strict as the cultural one.

I am not culturally American, but I like to arrive on time to appointments and events. This is my standard, and I adhere to it faithfully. I learned this in the United States Army since in Puerto Rico and in most Latin American countries timeliness is not a highly valued standard. I believe other people's time is as valuable as mine and I have to respect their time. But when my standard becomes an expectation of how other people should behave, I could feel anxious or angry if they fail to meet the expectation. My reasoning goes like this: I prefer that other people appreciate my time as being valuable. Everybody knows it is common sense to arrive at meetings on time (which of course is not true even if people thought it was common sense to be on time to meetings). Therefore, everybody should arrive to meetings on time.

The, so-called, common sense approach is not a standard that everybody shares. Who determines what common sense looks like? Sometimes common sense is not as common as some of us think. Many times, common sense is limited to an individual's perception of how things ought to be done.

Cultures can be identified by their shared values. It is those shared values that can be considered common sense within a particular context. However, individuals violate cultural customs all the time, and their reasons are more closely associated to their personal experiences than to their cultural influences. We need to be careful not to project our standards, developed as a result of our personal experiences, onto other people. When we avoid the emotional trap of projecting our standards onto others, we can curb our negative reactions to perceived failed expectations.

As stated earlier, expectations are personal standards applied to others. We have expectations of how other people should behave. These expectations are not always based on what we know about the person's character. They are normally based on our personal standard or simply a personal preference for these types of situations. Since standards are based on personal experience, it is not possible to expect that other people could meet our projection of the standard onto them. I will usually behave in ways that affirm as true what I have experienced as true in my life. An expectation demands that other people behave in the way I think they should behave. The problem is obvious. We cannot control how other people respond to situations because they have not shared all our life experiences.

Expectations have become so prevalent that some marriage counselors have designed sessions with the main goal of helping couples meet each other's expectations. The solution to this dilemma is readily apparent. Since in reality we cannot live up to other people's expectations, we should concentrate on living according to our standards without projecting them onto others. A wife cannot live according to a husband's expectations unless she knows his standard and vice versa. The ideal would be for husband and wife to share their preferences and then give their partners the freedom to find a way to meet the shared standard.

Iris and I were struggling with a couple of minor issues early on in our marriage. Iris could not, for the life of her, squeeze the paste tube from the bottom. And I could not push my dining table chair under the table after a meal. We were both frustrated with each other's behavior, but we could not figure out how to change the behavior or make the other change theirs. One day, I decided that since the tube paste was my issue, I would take the responsibility to fix the tube paste every day. After I made that choice, my frustrations ended, and I have not mentioned the issue to Iris again. She made the same decision regarding my inability to push the chair under the table, and she has lived happier ever since. The teaching point is that we can only control what we control, and fortunately that does not include our mates, friends, and associates, etc. This discussion about expectations is important because blind spots are the result of personal experiences we don't share with other people, but they produce in us expectations from others. Since the blind spot is mine, there is no conceivable way that another person can meet my expectations. This failure results in my instinctive reactivity against other people and situations.

Blind spots block people's ability to recognize the feelings associated with the original spiritual injury. This fact makes it imperative to step back and make an objective analysis, not of the original feelings, but of any reactions that may appear to be out of touch with the current event. Our primary concern cannot be about other people's reactions to the situations, but ours. Explaining other people's reactions does not help us identify our blinds spots. In the process to discover my blind spots, only my reactions are important. Additionally, we need to stay away from analyzing our reactions based on other people's behaviors, especially because their behaviors have nothing to do with my personal struggles. If we express any interest in other people's behavior it must be guided by a sincere commitment to contribute to their wellbeing. We can help others only when we illustrate their reactivity and compulsiveness without a judgmental or superior attitude. A positive attitude on our part can open the door for others to intervene with us in a positive and healthy way as well.

We can avoid many negative reactions to events by simply stopping the projection of our standards onto other people. Conversely, we can become more proactive in building relationships with others instead of waiting for negative actions to define our behavior. In the previous example about the issue of timeliness, we can share with our business associates our standard that we prefer to start our meetings in a timely manner. We can also tell them that we would appreciate a call if they fall behind schedule or are going to arrive late to accommodate their situation. With this approach, we let our associates know our standard for meetings, instead of trying to manipulate them into compliance. The healthier approach is to share our standards with others to encourage them to meet us half way and not to force compliance with a standard they probably do not share with us. Failure to conform to a standard is more due to lack of understanding than to an act of rebellion.

Personal standards are rules people develop through personal life experiences that have limited application. As such, my personal standards can be applied to other people when they choose to accept the reasoning behind it. This is not to say that we cannot have common standards, or that anarchy must reign. Nothing could be further from the truth. We need objective standards in a civil society, and this includes the church. The Bible provides objective principles by which we can measure our personal and social standards. Our personal standards differ from biblical principles in that the former are almost entirely based on family or cultural heritage. The latter are the result of divine revelation that takes place within a human context and are eternal in nature and scope. Revealed principles are inspired and take into account God's design for human nature. God, as the Creator of our nature, has exhaustive insight into our psychological make-up. Thus, a divinely revealed principle has inclusive application, i.e., they apply cross-culturally. Eternal principles do not differ from culture to culture in their day-to-day application. But cultural practices are exclusive to a culture and have limited application beyond that culture.

The biblical principle that men are "created in the image of God" means that every individual in every culture has God's imprint in their souls. This principle provides an objective standard by which we can judge people's dignity and worth—all of us have the same intrinsic worth before God. We are equally valuable, but we are not the same. This is the reason that divine principles serve as parameters that guide all human standards. We need to know that human standards are not equivalent nor are as authoritative as God's principles.

Therefore, when I am applying an eternal principle my primary task is to ensure that my understanding of the principle is as faithful to God's character as I can possibly make it. This is a key aspect of this argument. We cannot identify blind spots unless we have objective standards outside ourselves to measure our personal struggles. In other words, unless we know that God is the One that defines human dignity, we cannot know how abhorrent child abuse is to God. Whenever a society or cultural group takes God (the Christian God) out of the equation, all kinds of abuses against human dignity ensue. Take for example Muslim societies. They approved of two things we find criminal and morally corrupt: (1) slavery and (2) forcing girls as young as six years old to marry grown men. If a child's dignity has been violated, the damage can only be assessed as such if it is evaluated against an eternal principle that conforms to God's character.

As long as my personal standards conform to God's eternal principles, I will avoid unnecessary spiritual contradictions that may turn into spiritual injuries. Since an expectation, as defined earlier, is the projection of a personal standard onto other people, we will always be disappointed by other people's failures to meet our standards. However, if instead of projecting our expectations onto others we share our standards with them, people will be more sympathetic to our perspective. The same is true when we are willing to listen to other people's standards.

Third: Emotional Hot Buttons

A young mother said that her eighteen-month-old daughter would do certain things just to aggravate her. The mother felt that her baby was pushing her hot buttons intentionally. I was present when the mother made the statement, and since I know the mother fairly well, I asked her: "Do you really believe that your eighteen-months-old daughter gets up in the morning with the express purpose to make your day miserable?" She started laughing. Of course, she did not believe that. But there was something within her that reacted to her daughter's behavior. It would have been a good exercise for her to find out her blind spot so that she would not be as reactive to her daughter. The obvious issue here is that children that young do not know that their mothers have emotional hot buttons they can push. How do they know that their behaviors produce a predictable reaction by pushing their mothers' hot buttons? What are these buttons, anyway?

These so-called emotional buttons are blind spots finding expression in the parent's reactions to the child's behavior. If people are able to push our buttons on a regular basis and we continue to react in predictable ways, chances are good that we have let people know that we have blind spots. The apostle Paul encouraged children to respect their parents and for parents not to provoke their children to anger or not embitter them (Col. 3:19-21). Paul's words can be applied to the emotional manipulation that can take place between children and parents. These relationships are healthier and happier when they are not spending their time trying to take advantage of each other.

Another common expression says, "You are getting on my nerves." This is a different phrase with the same connotation. It should become clear that when our buttons are pushed and we are running out of patience, then something must be afoot. Pay attention to how easy people push your hot buttons or how easy they can "get on your nerves." These are good indicators that your emotions are not properly balanced as a result of a highly emotional event that makes you susceptible to manipulation. Something is out of kilter.

Fourth: Persistent Temptations

Another indicator that people have developed blind spots is evident when they consistently fall for similar temptations in specific areas of their lives. Please allow me to give a brief definition of temptation for this context. Temptation is not limited to sinful behavior. A temptation is the desire to engage in behaviors that are clearly unhealthy, or the inability to avoid falling for the same craving. There are two basic attitudes about temptations. The first attitude is from people that know when they are being tempted and make the conscious decision not to resist the temptation.

The second attitude about temptations is when people fail to recognize temptations for what they are—an enticement to violate God's character. People with blind spots can experience the same temptation a thousand times, recognize its dangers, and are still unable to prevent the fall or the subsequent shame associated with their susceptibility to it. They can see the temptation coming but feel impotent to overcome it. In either case, the temptation becomes clear after the fall. For example, a woman needs intimacy, but she has the tendency to enter relationships with abusive men, which are incapable to provide her with true emotional intimacy. Her desperate need for intimacy blinds her to the warning signs that she is about to connect with a man who has abusive tendencies. This means that her intimacy needs will remain unmet. She recognizes the man's abusive tendencies, but she is convinced that she can change him or manage the abuse because she has done it before. However, after the initial emotional attachment wears off she feels shame for making the same mistake once again. In some of the more dysfunctional cases, she may actually believe the lie that "this is what God wants for me."

Fifth: Inability to Complete Projects

A young man decided to join the United States Army. He was excited about his new life. Just before joining the army, he married his high school sweetheart so that she could follow him as soon as his basic training was over. His excitement came to a sudden end when, halfway into basic training, he quit. At the time of his decision, little did he know how this failure would become a spiritual injury that would mark him for life. For the rest of his life, that young man (now an aging man) has not been able to hold a job for more than two or three years at a time and finally ended up divorcing his wife. His failure to finish his military training and career became a metaphor for his life that turned into a vicious cycle of failure and incomplete results. The contradiction created by his failure with the army can be described thus:

His instinctive belief was that he was mentally and physically prepared to survive basic training. He should have made it. He was young enough and strong enough to make it with the rest of his class. His reality was that he failed in his basic training, and even though 90% of recruits pass without any problems, he was not able to accomplish what he believed he should have. This contradiction became the spiritual injury that altered his perception of self. He was no longer the confident young man that left his home for the army. In his mind, he had become a failure and his inability to finish basic training was his evidence. For many years, he was not able to think rationally about his military experience. Allow me to make three observations and three suggestions in this area to assist us move past similar issues.

A first observation is that a significant experience of failure has the tendency to create the resilient lie that we cannot be successful. The lie becomes the modus operandi (or our new truth), that can turn into a self-fulfilling prophecy. As long as people follow the lie, they will experience failure. This is not to say that they are incapable of success. Rather, people fail because they cannot visualize themselves succeeding in light of their initial failure. The lie affirms the failures, and every new failure reaffirms the lie. This is the classical vicious cycle.

Solution to the first observation: people have to replace the lie with a truth in order to change the self-fulfilling prophecy cycle.

A second observation is that a significant experience of failure can create mistrust of our own giftedness. That is, we could believe that we failed because our talents and gifts let us down. We could become reluctant to depend on our gifts and talents. One of the consequences is that we don't believe in the sufficiency of our giftedness. The issue here is that if people cannot trust their own giftedness, they cannot achieve anything. Losing confidence in our gifts is an indication that we can no longer see God's glory manifested in them.

Solution to the second observation: people have to rebuild the concept of God's image in them. God loves us. God created us in his image with all the benefits that entails. Until people are confident and able to experience God's image in them, they will flounder aimlessly.

A final observation is that the lie and the personal mistrust could result in a deeply rooted perception of low self-esteem. This type of low self-esteem is more than just a poor perception of self. This type of low self-esteem robs people of their dignity and becomes a determining factor in how they relate to other people and God. There is a sense that people have lost all sense of self-worth. Another expression of this type of low self-esteem is our tendency to lash out in anger at people every time anything threatens our comfort zone.

Solution to the final observation: people can rebuild their self-esteem by focusing on the inherent value that God has placed on each one of them. That is, instead of believing the lie, people could focus their energies in reinforcing the truth that their worth comes from God and no man can take it from them. People's worthiness is determined by God's love and not by men's approval. God loves them to the point of sending his only Son to rescue them from the hell of an existence without God. That is, God has valued them so highly that he decided to take upon himself the scorn that broke our relationship with him. If God loves us so, we need to change how we evaluate our self-worth to include God's opinion on the matter.

Let me summarize this chapter. Catastrophic spiritual injuries are the result of an inherent irreconcilable contradiction between what a person believes to be true and what is actually true. The result of these contradictions is that they produce an invisible spiritual pain in people's souls. Spiritual injuries leave spiritual scars that turn into blind spots when people create a lie to survive the trauma. These blind spots are emotional *gaps* (a vacuum of feelings) in the intimacy mechanism that could make people susceptible to temptations from within and without, while preventing them from engaging in healthy intimate relationships with God and others. These blind spots could make people susceptible to manipulation and control by others. The best way to identify blind spots is to watch for the following behavioral patterns: (1) susceptibility to similar types of temptations, (2) susceptibility to being manipulated by others, (3) instinctive reactivity to certain events or people.

After years of habit-forming behaviors, it is very difficult to recognize people's instinctive reactions to circumstances. They need other people's help to recognize the instinctive reactions and the temptations to which they can so easily succumb. All behavioral patterns have a cause. People need to know these patterns in order to search for their initial cause. Understanding their behaviors will help people accept the presence of blind spots, which in turn can help them recognize the trauma that produced the original spiritual injury or the original irreconcilable contradiction. Once people have identified these patterns in their conduct, they can finally enter into the healing process.

I need to give one more word of caution. We cannot engage people's reactivity without their permission. That is, the fact that I may have noticed reactivity and defensiveness on someone does not authorize me to become their counselor or their conscience. If we notice that a friend shows signs of instinctive reactivity, we should ask their permission before we start pointing out the issue because we don't know how complicated this issue could turn out to be. We can say something like this: "Matt, can I make an observation? I noticed that you became very defensive when Joe said this or that. Have you noticed if this is a pattern in how you respond to situations?" If permission is granted, we may have gained a friend. If permission is not granted, silence is the better part of wisdom.

CHAPTER 4

Family Secrets: Hidden in Plain Sight

Maria entered my office in a state of panic and hysteria. She had to go home, she told me. She was almost incoherent and was clearly distraught. Since we were in a military deployment outside the country, allowing her to go home was not an easy decision to make. In order for me to help her, I needed to have a compelling reason to present to the commander to see if he could honor her request to go home. Her initial statement was not very convincing. She said that her grandfather was coming to her hometown for a visit. While I appreciated the desire to be home for her grandfather's visit, I could not in good conscience recommend her to leave. Her explanation did not meet the army's criteria to be released from her deployment.

Maria's next statement gave me the first clue that I was in for a rough session. She stated that her six-year old daughter was staying with her mother and it was important for her to go home. It dawned on me that this young mother did not want to go home to greet her grandfather. She needed to go home to protect her daughter from her grandfather. I asked her to be as candid as possible in order for me to make a good case to secure the commander's approval.

Maria told me the following story. Including her mother, her grandparents had eight daughters. Maria's grandfather had sexually molested all his eight daughters. She added that the daughters had procreated twelve granddaughters and, according to her, he had molested all twelve including Maria. I was stunned by her revelation. Even if half of her story was true, I had to find a way to convince the commander to let her go home. She said, "He did it to me and to everyone else, but if he touches my daughter, I will kill him with my own hands." Her anger and frustration felt very real to me. She would not stay still and even suggested that she would leave the country without permission if she had to.

I asked her if her grandmother knew about the systematic abuse by the grandfather. Maria said the grandmother knew and all the daughters knew, but that no one would dare say anything. Even Maria's mother had made excuses for her grandfather's behavior by saying, "Well, that's just the way he is." Maria added that this was a family secret that everyone knew, but no one wanted to talk about it. She had promised herself that she would not, under any circumstances, allow her grandfather to touch her daughter. After such a horrific story, I had no choice but to ask the commander to approve Maria's request to return home. She left the country the very next day, and I still pray that she made it home safely and on time. I will probably never see Maria again, but I hope that her daughter grew up spiritually healthy and happy.

When families discourage transparency, they will keep secrets that hurt every member of the family, even if they are not aware of how the damage will manifest itself in the future. As many have said, "sunshine is the best of disinfectants."[15] Transparency does not hide or excuse dysfunctional behaviors. It serves as insulation from predators. Children feel safer when they can trust their parents, and they are healthier when the family unit discourages damaging family secrets. The power of shame is in keeping the family secret.

Catastrophic spiritual injuries have three distinct symptoms: (1) false shame, (2) false guilt, and (3) loss of trust. In order to get people past these three destructive consequences, we need to identify the circumstances that give them legitimacy as well as the instinctive reactiveness that is used to cover up the pain caused by the original spiritual injury. Over the rest of this chapter, I will take a look at these three symptoms, and offer a few suggestions that may give hope to the injured person to overcome their damaging impacts. First, let me define healthy shame to facilitate our discussion on false shame.

---

[15] Louis D. Brandeis, (1856-1941). Former Associate Justice of the United States Supreme Court.

Healthy Shame

The biblical model that reveals the issues shame is found in the story of Adam and Eve in the Garden of Eden. God created Adam and Eve and "they were naked and felt no shame" (Gen. 3:27). Adam and Eve had nothing to hide before God. Their *nakedness* was not only the physical condition in which they lived in the Garden of Eden, it was also a metaphor for their transparent relationship the first couple enjoyed with God. The *fall* opened their eyes and they became aware of their nakedness that found expression as both guilt for their willful disobedience against God and shame for the ugliness the new sinful condition produced that became a barrier to their fellowship with God. The immediate consequence of Adam's and Eve's sin was an uncontrollable desire to hide from God. Their impulsive reaction to escape from God's presence was their spiritual recognition that their actions were unacceptable to God. In a very real sense, we are still hiding from God to this day.

After the first couple disobeyed God's commandment, they felt embarrassed to be in God's presence. Something had changed in their natures that made them repellent to God, even if God had not made such a statement. Their rebellion had obscured their ability to identify God's image in them and they became God's enemies in their minds (Col. 1:21). They had abandoned their initial state of innocence and "discovered that they were naked," which meant that they were no longer free to fellowship with God with honesty of heart. In other words, they realized their sin had broken their fellowship with God and in spite of their compulsive desire to hide their sin from God they could not.

Adam and Eve were created in God's image, but after their disobedience, sin distorted God's image in them. They had lost their source of self-worth. The serpent offered them to become like God, but Adam and Eve were not able to discern the serpent's deception. They were already in the image of God. The serpent's deception was in that it offered them something they already had. Our creation in God's image gave us intrinsic value as persons, for we shared in God's personhood qualities, and no one has the right to distort or steal this value from us. It follows that when God's image in us was distorted by sin, as it happened in the Garden of Eden, our intrinsic self-worth was devalued, and shame became our *nakedness.*

When Adam and Eve lost their standing before God, they also lost the freedom to be in God's presence, but not because God had rejected them. Rather, they surrendered to the serpent their right to fellowship with God. Their natural response to their shame was to hide from God to cover their newfound and embarrassing nakedness. They felt shame for personal behavior that displeased God. This type of shame led them to repentance. Their first reaction to cover their shame by hiding from God's presence was a good indicator that their intimacy mechanism was still functional. God will heal our spiritual injuries, but we need to stop hiding. In order for us to overcome our shame, we have to expose its source. As long as we continue to cover our shame, we will not be able to address the spiritual injury which is responsible for the dysfunctional intimacy mechanism.

As mentioned earlier, shame loses its power when people expose the events or the circumstances that produced it. That is, when people confess to God the sin that birthed their shame, they defang the negative power shame holds over them. In turn, coming to terms with their personal sin is the first step to restore trust, which is the initial and essential step to repair the intimacy mechanism. Once people realize that they no longer have to hide from God regardless of their behavior, the injury is exposed and the feelings of being inadequate begin to be removed. This is possible only because God has accepted them unconditionally based on the sacrificed Jesus made on the cross.

There are several reasons the Lord encourages people to stay "in the vine" (Jn. 15:5-8). If they are going to survive, fellowship with Jesus is a non-negotiable element of the equation. The Church is also described as the Body of Christ to symbolize the unity that should exist among the believers (1 Cor. 12:27). However, that's not the only function of a body. The body also has self-healing and sustaining qualities that must also be present in the Body of Christ. The writer of the book of Hebrews discouraged believers from "forsaking the assembly" (Heb. 10:25). I believe coming together in worship in the assembly, is people's entry way to knowing God's character, and to begin the process of healing only the community of faith can produce. James affirmed this truth when he stated that,

> "Is any one of you sick? He should call the elders of the church to pray over him and anoint him with oil in the name of the Lord. And the prayer offered in faith will make the sick person well; the Lord will raise him up. If he has sinned, he will be forgiven. Therefore, confess your sins to each other and pray for each other so that you may be healed. The prayer of a righteous man is powerful and effective" (Jam. 5:14-16).

One of Satan's strategies is to shame people so that they cannot enter into God's presence with confidence. If people are not in fellowship with God and the church, the devil can destroy their witness to the world as God's ambassadors. Needless to say, people's fellowship with God is the prerequisite to an effective witness. When the devil can keep people ashamed to be in God's presence, they will not even be able to pray effectively. This type of shame also keeps people away from the fellowship with other believers who can play a key role in their spiritual health journey. The church is our place of refuge, but if we stay away from the assembly, we lose our intimacy with God and fellowship with the community of faith. The psalmist said it best: "God is our refuge in the time of trouble..." (Ps. 61:3; 62:7; 62:8). Whenever we make a mistake or inflict an injury on others, the best thing to do is show empathy for others and accept the healthy shame that can bring reconciliation and restoration.

Shame Based Behavior

Most people do not know why they feel so unworthy. One contributing factor could be people's inability to identify the circumstances that produce the false shame. If individuals feel shame but do not know why, they may carry a feeling of unworthiness for someone else's behavior. Their failure to recognize that their unworthiness is based on a false sense of shame becomes a hindrance in placing the blame where it belongs—either in the event or in the person that caused the spiritual injury. In many instances, people's actions to cover the false shame have the opposite effect, exposing them to growing feelings of unworthiness.

FAMILY SECRETS: HIDDEN IN PLAIN SIGHT

False shame enslaves people to the spiritual injury that produced the shame. As long as the feelings of shame persist, the frequency or the intensity of the self-destructive behaviors, in an attempt to cover the shame, will continue to increase. The reason for this increase in intensity is that as people grow older, they become weary of carrying the weight of the false shame that has burdened them for most of their lives. Additionally, the increased intensity of shame may result in feelings of hopelessness because people cannot find a way out of their sense of unworthiness. Some people believe that if they were able to change the behavior associated with the shame, they could eliminate feeling unworthy. Unfortunately, this reasoning does not produce lasting results. Shame-based behavior is the result of a lie that victims of traumatic events are responsible for their victimization. Until the lie is exposed and defanged with the truth, the individuals trapped by the lie cannot get rid of their feelings of shame. The fact that people can make external behavioral changes does not eliminate the feelings of unworthiness produced by the false shame. I would suggest that the antidote to false shame cannot be found through external behavioral changes. We need to place the shame squarely on the people that caused the spiritual injury. For instance, victims of rape must identify the rapist as the one responsible for the spiritual injury. The predators should be the ones feeling shame for their behavior.

This is not to say that these external changes are not necessary. But, the most effective changes are made after people recognize the source of their false sense of shame and have shifted the blame from themselves onto the perpetrators, where it belongs. The external changes are also necessary to give individuals a new sense of achievement that facilitates replacing the lie with the truth. Please understand that unless the false shame-based behavior is properly addressed, the process to heal the spiritual injury will be much slower and more painful.

Shame and Sexual Dysfunction

I will make two statements that I have seen as experientially true, even though many would object to the conclusions. Shame based behavior is almost always connected to *relational* spiritual injuries.

This means that many of the adults who experience shame-based behaviors have been abused as children. This systematic abuse has caused several types of dysfunctions in their relationships with people of the opposite sex. Their emotional intimacy needs are as strong as the needs of the rest of the population, but since their intimacy mechanism was damaged during childhood, they live with an unbalance view of intimacy that leads some to sexual aversion, and others to sexual promiscuity. Very rarely do these people have a balance and healthy expression of their sexual intimacy. These individuals were traumatized during a time in which they did not have the mental and emotional coping skills to understand or to manage the intrusion of an adult into their private places.

The violence experienced by these children begins to manifest very early in their lives through dysfunctional sexual relationships. They would have the tendency to define intimacy, solely, based on sexual activity and, as a result, they view people as sexual predators or sexual victims. The individuals functioning from a shame-based sexuality will have the tendency to distance themselves emotionally from their partners, or they would function with an out of control libido that drives them into multiple sexual encounters if single, or into multiple extra marital affairs if married.

On the one hand, we find that some of these individuals desire healthy intimacy, but since they define intimacy from the perspective of the dirtiness of sexual intercourse, they are repulsed by their sexual activity, even after they have been married for years. On the other hand, we find cases, like the woman who had been married for over twenty years with the same man, but who had maintained sexual affairs with acquaintances, coworkers, and other married men for the totality of her married life. Her reasoning was that she needed continuous sexual activity to keep her marriage vibrant and viable. Her husband, as far as she could tell, never knew of her extra marital engagements.

Please understand that I am not claiming that everyone, in every place, and at all times have the same experiences. My conclusions are the result of thirty-eight years of counseling couples and individuals in all types of family conflicts and dysfunctions and three years of experience in a psychiatric treatment facility in which we observed over 2,700 patients with addictive behaviors. Every one of the patients

I saw had experienced, what I define in this book, as a catastrophic spiritual injury.

Susan told me she had married a good man. He was very understanding, but from the very beginning of their marriage they had suffered from sexual problems. She wanted to be with him when he was not home, but as soon as he would arrive at the house, her desire for intimacy would turn from wanting to be with her husband to wanting to sleep in a separate room. They had three children, and she submitted to sexual activity with her husband because she loved him, and she believed it was part of the marriage arrangement, but she could not become emotionally engaged.

Her struggle was more painful because when her husband was working or away from home, all she could think about was how to have a healthy and strong sexual relationship with him. After fifteen years she realized that something needed to change. She specifically stated that her husband had never cheated on her, but she was getting more concerned that, after years of frustration and rejection, he might choose that option. So, she asked me if I knew of anything she could do to resolve her conflict of desiring sexual intimacy with her husband, while hating the very thought.

I asked her if she knew why she felt shame of being sexually active with her husband. In one of those rare cases, she knew exactly what was happening. She said that she had always seen sex as dirty and embarrassing. Obviously, I had to ask how did she arrive at that conclusion, since God himself created sex and he did not seem embarrassed by it. She was a little stunned by my statement. She told me she had never considered that possibility, but she still could not help feeling dirty. I asked her again, how did she reach this conclusion? Her face turned somber and tears began to flow down her cheeks. After a couple of minutes, she told me her story.

Susan began by saying that she had never told anyone what she was about to tell me. I remained silent. Then, she said that her step father had sexually abused her from the time she was eight to the time she was fifteen. After she turned fifteen, her stepfather moved to her sister who was six years younger than her. She knew he was also abusing her sister because she could hear her cry often, but at the time all she could think about was that she was grateful that it was no longer her. After graduating from high school Susan left the house for college and decided she was going to expose this family secret. She reported the abuse and had her sister removed from her mother's home. The stepfather was incarcerated, but her mother never forgave her for *destroying* her marriage. Now, at the age of thirty-five Susan was still looking for a solution to her shame to save her marriage.

The tragedy of this story is that it is so common that many women reading this would think that I am talking about them. But Susan is a real person who suffered the indignity of a vicious pedophile for seven years in her own home. She brought her husband for a few more sessions and they were able to confront the sexual abuse. They made some choices that could help them begin the healing process to repair their intimacy. As it happens with the army, I moved to another post and never saw them again. I pray they were able to find some peace of mind that would allow them to escape from the viciousness of the shame-based behavior that had plagued their marriage.

The intimacy dysfunction resulting from sexual abuse manifests, primarily, in two ways. In Susan's case, the sexual dysfunction manifested in sexual aversion, even though she still had the natural need for sexual intimacy with her husband. On the other case I mentioned above, the intimacy dysfunction was expressed in compulsive sexual relationships. Some people call this sexual addiction. I want to make clear that not everyone who engages in multiple relationships over the years is sexually addicted. In this context, I am limiting this description to people who engage in compulsive sexual activity as a substitute for their basic need for emotional and spiritual intimacy in a monogamous relationship. It is also important to note that not everyone who engages in promiscuous sexual activity has been sexually abused. But when sexual promiscuity is present, we must ask the question about sexual abuse just in case there is a need to assist the person through a spiritual healing process.

False Shame

According to the popular poem *My Name is Toxic Shame* by Leo Booth and John Bradshaw, shame is the "voracious hole that fuels all addictions." Shame and addictions go hand in hand.[16] This problem is even more pronounced when people must keep the secret of their victimization because the predator has imposed a false sense of shame on the victim.

I know many cultures define shame differently. But even if shame is absolutely limited to nurture, the acknowledgement of its existence confirms my assertion that shame is a part of the human consciousness and it cannot be evaluated through any scientific method. But regardless of the source, the fact remains that this non-material element is as real to us as our own flesh. Most people know that their experiences, both physical and spiritual, are interconnected and they influence how we interact with the world around us, and how we relate with other people. For example: fear causes many people to break into heavy sweating, or it accelerates their heart rate, or in some cases some people even faint, etc. Thus, fear which is a non-physical experience can produce physical reactions in most people. Fear, like many other spiritual responses to emotional events is both, physically testable and experientially undeniable. It is physically testable because the physical symptoms are easily recognizable. And it's experientially undeniable because of the physical reaction it produces.

Shame combines feelings of dishonor, unworthiness, and embarrassment. When people feel unworthy, they have the tendency to self-medicate to survive the shame to be found in public with other people. I can mention two basic expressions of shame. First, when shame is the result of personal sin and it leads to repentance, it can have a healing effect. Feeling shame for personal sin is an indication that the intimacy mechanism is functioning properly. That is, it is perfectly consistent to feel embarrassed if we have done a shameful thing. The basic Biblical teaching regarding shame is found in Genesis 2:25. The first couple "were both naked and felt no shame." Adam and Eve were completely exposed in God's presence. They had no reason to hide from God and thus, there was no need to feel shame. After the fall, their rebellion against God produced a shame that turned into fear of being in his presence (Gen.

---

[16] Caroline Shaw. The Toxic Mix of Shame and Addiction. The Clearing, (May 16, 2016).

3:10). Healthy shame is always an expression of personal sin, and a healthy resolution is repentance and reconciliation. This means that people do not hide their shameful conduct, and upon repentance, they feel accepted again. It is very possible that acceptance is the most fundamental aspect of the restoration process. Whenever people commit personal sins and do not feel shame, they are either in denial of the consequences of their sins or they have lost the moral compass that assists them in deciding between right and wrong. Adam and Eve were ashamed of who they had become in their attempt to live independently of God, which is the ultimate expression of sin.

The Encyclopedia of Christianity defines sin as "any lack of conformity, active or passive, to the moral law of God. This may be a matter of act, of thought, or of inner disposition or state."[17] Ravi Zacharias defined sin as "the violation of the person of God."[18] R.C. Sproul wrote of sin:

> In the least transgression I set myself above the authority of God, doing insult to His majesty, His holiness, and His sovereign right to govern me. Sin is a revolutionary act in which the sinner seeks to depose God from His throne. Sin is a presumption of supreme arrogance in that the creature vaunts his own wisdom above that of the Creator, challenges divine omnipotence with human impotence, and seeks to usurp the rightful authority of the cosmic Lord.[19]

Sin can be defined as any behavior or thought that places man at the center of adoration and robs God of his place as the Sovereign Ruler over the universe. Whenever individuals act in such a way that they violate God's moral law, they should feel shame for their behaviors. God's moral law establishes the standard for conduct, and people should know the difference between good and evil. This was one of the main points of the Genesis narrative in which Adam

---

[17] Encyclopedia of Christianity. Definition of Sin.

[18] Ravi Zacharias. What is Sin? https://www.youtube.com/watch?v=RIcPO1TVohM

[19] R. C. Sproul. The Holiness of God. https://www.goodreads.com/quotes/428210-sin-is-cosmic-treason-sin-is-treason-against-a-perfectly

and Eve rebelled against God. Before their sin they were "naked and felt no shame." After their sin, they "discovered they were naked and hid themselves from God." This is the nature of sin—it exposes our evil by the light of God's holiness. When people feel shame for personal sins, their intimacy mechanism is working properly, which is a needed element for repentance and reconciliation.

Elwell and Comfort defined sin as "evildoing that is not only against humanity, society, others, or oneself, but against God."[20] Jefford, in his definition in the Eerdmans' dictionary, stated that sin is "a reality signifying the broken relationship between God and humanity. The occasions by which this relationship breaks, the need to recognize this rupture, and the avenues for salvation are detailed in endless situations throughout the Scriptures."[21] Sin is a betrayal of a formerly established relationship. Once there has been a break in the relationship, the parties must reconcile in order to heal the rift and restore intimacy between the parties.

The second expression of shame is more complicated. It is called false shame. We addressed false shame in earlier paragraphs, but I would like to expand further. False shame is not directly related to any personal sinful behaviors, and as a result, it cannot lead to repentance and restoration. A person cannot repent for something for which they are not directly responsible. It is not healthy or helpful to apologize for someone else's sins. It is even more harmful to assume the shame for someone else's behavior. Either one of these options could become a spiritual injury by creating an irreconcilable contradiction. It is simply not congruent to accept blame for other people's actions, regardless of how insignificant they might be.

For example, if a woman feels ashamed for being a sexual abuse victim as a child, she is experiencing false shame. Her shame is entirely the result of the perpetrator's manipulation. Though she has not personally done anything, she blames herself for the abuse,

---

[20]   Elwell, W. A., & Comfort, P. W. (2001). In *Tyndale Bible dictionary* (Wheaton, IL: Tyndale House Publishers), p. 1203.

[21]   C. N. Jefford, (2000). Sin. In D. N. Freedman, A. C. Myers, & A. B. Beck (Eds.), (*Eerdmans dictionary of the Bible*, Grand Rapids, MI: W.B. Eerdmans), p. 1224.

faulting her own character or her physical appearance. She could feel as damaged goods and unlovable. She cannot even begin to heal from the feelings of worthlessness until she recognizes that the shame she feels for her victimization is false. The shame she feels is a byproduct of her defilement and not the result of any bad deeds that originated with her. She feels violated and powerless to change her feelings in light of the violence perpetrated against her.

Her shame is false because there is no direct correlation between any behavior on her part and the shame. If she is going to heal, she must come to terms with the truth that she was not responsible for the violence she suffered. The perpetrator's behavior does not, in any spiritual way, damage God's image in her. However, he might have created the perception that her dignity has been taken from her. As a child she did not have the information or the spiritual maturity to overcome the perpetrator's lies. So, she internalized the violence by reasoning that there must be something wrong with her. Therefore, as long as she feels responsible for the violence, she will continue to blame herself for the trauma, and the false shame will persist. She needs to stop evaluating her dignity through the perpetrator's behavior. The perpetrator's shameful behavior is the reason for her shame, not the standard for it.

The presence of false shame always results in the loss of self-worth. The person feels less valuable as a result of the event that caused the spiritual injury. As the reader may have inferred, not all spiritual injuries lead to false shame, even if all of them do permanent damage to the intimacy mechanism. False shame comes from relational spiritual injuries that attack the person's dignity and self-worth by demeaning their value. Often these spiritual injuries are in the form of persistent physical, psychological, and sexual abuse. Let me make a clarification at this point. When I use the phrase relational spiritual injuries, I am referring to the type of trauma caused by someone we would normally associate with trust and emotional intimacy, such as a father, mother, uncles, aunts, teachers, family friends, or other person we would normally believe should protect us. Instead of receiving love and care from these individuals, the person received abuse and neglect. Instead of feeling safe with them, they rob us of our safety in the intimacy of our homes, schools, and neighborhoods.

False shame adds the false belief that the individual has become unworthy to be loved. It is often the leading cause for the loss of self-esteem. When our dignity is violated, we will find ourselves between the proverbial rock and a hard place. On the one hand, we cannot get rid of the feelings of unworthiness. On the other, we have a very difficult time offering forgiveness to an unrepentant perpetrator. People have to change both circumstances. They have to reject the shame produced by the victimization, and they have to work to rid themselves of the hatred and resentment the violation of trust left behind. This process makes it crucial to identify, as early as possible, what type of shame people are experiencing to take the proper approach to correct the problem.

False shame, as seen above, creates a separate set of issues. Imagine the consequences of feeling embarrassed, dirty, and worthless because of a perpetrator's behavior. There is no repentance for false shame because the victim cannot repent for someone else's violence. When a spiritual injury produces false shame, the first step in the healing process must be to properly identify the source of the trauma. Otherwise, the healing process will be delayed until the injured person is able to regain a feeling of worthiness through years of counseling and self-reconciliation. To get this process going I suggest a two steps process.

The first step to solve her feelings of false shame is to change her perspective. She has to name her perpetrator and define the events from the correct perspective. That is, she must recognize that her perpetrator is the shameless SOB that injured her. She did not bring this trauma upon herself. The perpetrator is the one responsible for the violence, the trauma, and the violation of her privacy. And she must confront the perpetrator with this truth. This confrontation is not a violent or even a face to face encounter. It could take many forms, especially since most perpetrators are family members or family friends. The initial stage is writing a letter detailing the event to let the perpetrator know that she no longer blames herself for his actions. Once she has digested this truth, she can send the letter to the perpetrator so that he would know that she is no longer a victim of his actions. If there were other people that covered up or facilitated the perpetrator's behavior, she will send them the letter as well. If the perpetrator is dead, she would take the letter to his grave and read it there as a symbolic act that she is breaking his grip on her shame.

The second step is to rediscover that, in spite of her circumstances, God is the source of her dignity. She might have blamed God for abandoning her during her most difficult moments, but God is not responsible for humanity's violence and depravity. Most people think that since God is omnipotent, he should have done something. But, and this is a crucial aspect of our lives on this earth, God does not always interfere with people free expression of their freewill. He created us with the capacity to make free moral choices, and in spite of the issues this brings, he is committed to let the sinful condition be fully manifested in our lives. We could prefer that the world was different, but this is the best world in which we can find redemption, because without the full manifestation of sin and shame, we would not seek to renew our relationship with God.

Since the healing process often involves several steps functioning at the same time, we need to be prepared for the inevitable appearance of false shame. When the person has experienced a relational spiritual injury, which is what sexual victimization is, it is almost inevitable that the victim will experience false shame. It is necessary to identify false shame as early in the healing process as possible. Otherwise, people might be fighting to heal from an injury while guarding a secret produced by false shame. Their ability to quickly identify the source of the false shame allows the injured person to change the lie about their worthlessness for the truth that their dignity is not dependent on the perpetrator's opinion or actions. Individuals who are able to resolve the issues of false shame quickly are also able to manage their blind spots more effectively. Even when low self-esteem persists, we can make major progress as soon as we are able to eliminate the lie that produced the false sense of shame.

The Cycle of Shame

Orlando was the father of a childhood friend. As long as I could remember he was an alcoholic. After many years of alcohol and psychological abuse, his wife decided to take her two youngest children with her and move to New York. The oldest child stayed with the father for about another year. One day in a drunken rage, the father kicked his oldest son out of the house. The son left Puerto Rico and moved to New York with his mother. Orlando knew about my friendship with his son, and from time to time he would ask me to write letters to his son. I wrote the letters to his oldest son at least twice a month.

Whenever Orlando received a letter from the oldest son, I would read them to him. The pattern went like this for several months. Orlando was becoming more and more depressed because of his son's absence. He constantly blamed himself and his drinking for losing his family, and finally for losing his oldest son. One day I went to the house to write Orlando's letter to his son, but there was a lot of commotion outside the house. When I arrived, I saw that Orlando had taken his life. He was not able to overcome the guilt and shame he felt for rejecting the only son that had chosen to stay with him. He had lost his will to live, and he reached the point of no return. This was the tragic ending of a life that drowned itself in alcohol. Orlando reached rock bottom and when he found himself without hope, he took his own life.

For every Orlando that ends in suicide, there are millions that just drift through life suffering from an incurable spiritual pain filled with guilt and shame. They live in constant fear of facing their spiritual pain and cannot see any alternatives to escape it.

I believe the church can play a larger role as a healing agent in our communities. Some of the old methods of just telling people *to get over it* have to be replaced with a more loving fellowship in which God is glorified in our worship and people can experience acceptance as they are. Acceptance is the best approach to gain the trust of the brokenhearted. There is healing in the community of faith. The Lord left us a means of grace in the Communion celebration. When we break bread together, we remember Jesus's gift of life to us and we share God's grace with one another. Breaking bread together is a marvelous occasion to find acceptance and reconciliation!

Once people have hit rock bottom as a result of self-destructive behaviors, the first step in the healing process is no longer discovering the original spiritual injury. Rather, the first step is to defeat the addiction. The addiction becomes the new reality in a desperate attempt to cover the damage produced by the false sense of guilt and shame. The addictions play a negative role in people's perception of self. As long as the addiction defines who people have become, they would not be able to escape their rock bottom. The key to escaping rock bottom is to realize that the addiction does not have the final say in determining people's worth.

When people recognize and reject the lie that their self-worth is determined by their addictions, they are in a position to regain a healthier perception of self that can open the door to spiritual healing. People cannot undo the chain of events created by the spiritual injury. However, they can slow down or even reverse the consequences of the spiritual injury when they brake the power grip the addiction has over them. The victory over the self-destructive behavior opens the door of restoration to fellowship with God and other.

Cycle of Shame Exposed

A stepfather had systematically abused his wife's three daughters. He abused them in turns. First it was the six-year-old. He abused her until she was about twelve. Then, when the three-year-old girl turned six, he started abusing her. Finally, when the one-year-old turned six, it was her turn. The older girl realized her stepfather's tactic after her middle sister began complaining to her about the abuse. She became concerned for her younger sister. She knew that once she turned six, the stepfather would also abuse her, too. She was very scared. Finally, the older sister told her mother of the predatory behaviors of the stepfather, but the mother sided with her husband and basically left the girls to fend for themselves under those circumstances.

The abuse continued for years until the middle girl ran away from home at fourteen years of age and went to the police. The stepfather was arrested, and after much questioning, he was charged with multiple counts of sexual abuse, aggravated assault, and rape. During the investigation, the police discovered that the mother was aware of the abuse, but she had allowed the abuse to go on to *save* her marriage and the family. The mother was also arrested on similar charges. The damage done to those girls cannot be measured. If the mother had acted the first time, she would have spared her daughters from the hands of the vicious predator she had brought into her home. Parents must encourage an environment of trust and transparency to give their children the freedom to come forth when something is not proper.

We have presented transparency as the foundation upon which we can build the process to heal our deepest spiritual injuries. The reason transparency plays such a big role in the spiritual healing process is that until we are able to recognize and expose sin for what it is, we will not be able to address its devastating consequences. A damaging family secret is created when family members imitate Adam's statement in the Garden of Eden: "I realized I was naked, and I was afraid to be in your presence." That is, the family chooses to put the dysfunction in the spiritual closet. There, the secret is safe from coming to light, and everybody can go on living as if the secret did not exist. But the people damaged by the dysfunction will also remain trapped in the dark closet.

When a shameful act is committed within a family unit, we can take two basic actions. (1) We can expose the act and make its future manifestation more difficult, or (2) we can hide the act and pretend that it never happened. The former attitude brings transparency to the problem that allows healing. The latter attitude perpetuates the dysfunction by refusing to address the conditions and the context that allowed the injury to occur. King David chose the first option and confessed before God. But Adam and Eve chose the more damaging second option and hid from God.

Revealing a dysfunctional family secret is not easy. There is plenty of pressure not to betray the family unit. If the secret gets out, the family may not survive (and most people are unwilling to deal with that possibility). There is, however, one way to know whether a family has a dysfunctional secret. The presence of a *black sheep* within the family unit is a good indicator that the family may have a secret that no one dares speak out loud. The *black sheep* becomes the carrier of the family's dysfunctional secret. In return for his sacrifice, the family focuses its attention in the care of the *black sheep* to protect the rest of the family from the hidden dysfunction. Finally, the *black sheep* becomes the family's identified patient, and everyone is responsible to protect him because he does not know any better. This arrangement works fairly well until one of the members of the family decides to abandon ship. They do not approve of the dysfunction, or the black sheep's behavior, and are unwilling to spend their lives caring for the identified patient. Once one member of the family breaks the cycle of codependency, the rest of the family falls apart and the *black sheep* is left to fend for himself, something he has failed to do his entire life.

If people are ignorant of the scope of God's omniscience, they will do whatever they have to in order to hide from his piercing eyes. Eventually people find out that all their efforts only served to keep them separated from God. This is when the "chickens come home to roost." At this stage, people are no longer able to deny the pain associated with the spiritual injury, or they find themselves so far removed from the event that caused the original injury that they can no longer make the connection between the injury and the pain. Failure to make the connection between the pain and the spiritual injury could result in a much longer healing process because the person does not know what they are looking for. People need to simply refuse to cover up for perpetrators. The decision to expose the perpetrators will take away their ability to play their vicious game.

As we have stated, shame thrives in secrecy. Diana Hardy once said that, "Whether man or beast, the secrets you kept in the fathoms of your heart always held you to ransom."[22] When the secrets are hiding a violent dysfunction in which abuse is persistent, the secret becomes the first line of defense for the predator. Patti Feuereisen shared that exposing the secret of her molestation could have prevented many years of guilt and shame. Read her words with me.

---

[22]   Dianna Hardy. Reign of the Wolf. Kindle Edition by Satin Smoke Press, 2017.

At the time I was being molested, I thought I was the only one. My father controlled everything in our house and he always said that what was happening to me was natural and that I should accommodate him. Even though I have to look back sometimes, I am moving forward. And even though it's painful for me to face my mother's complacency, doing so has helped me understand that it wasn't my fault. If I could have read something at the time about sex abuse, if people had talked openly about, I could have been saved so many years of guilt and shame and secrecy. Each time I talk about my incest, I get rid of some of that shame and guilt. Each person I share with, no matter what their response, takes another piece of the pain away.[23]

Overcoming Shame

King David's example, cited above, demonstrates the instinctive reaction people have if they feel their shame is about to be exposed. When we make a mistake, or if we injure someone, or if we sin against God, our instinctive tendency is to respond like Adam and Eve, to hide. They "discovered" they were naked. They had sinned before a holy God. It was this self-realization that embarrassed them. Something had changed in their psychological make-up. They had violated God's commands and were no longer "comfortable" or "worthy" to be in God's presence. God did not have to tell them that. They knew it instinctively.

King David's reaction to his sin was similar to Adam and Eve. The difference was that King David reacted to what he thought was someone else's sin, instead of his own. But when the prophet revealed that David, himself, was the guilty party, he was devastated by what he had done against Uriah and against God. For David, as well as for the rest of us, the process to overcoming shame is to come clean. That is, it all begins with transparency (confession) and repentance

---

[23]   Patty Feuereisen. Invisible Girls: The Truth About Sexual Abuse. Seal Press, 2005.

(turning away from the shameful behavior) and surrendering to God's grace. Let me share three suggestions to overcome shame.

Let me clarify that these are not salvation steps. They are part of the process that helps people grow in their transparency and intimacy with God. We already know that salvation is the result of God's grace revealed to us in Christ and we receive God's gift of life through faith. The point here is that to be transparent before God is not an easy task even after he has changed our standing before him. We were God's enemies, but we are now reconciled and at peace with him (Rom. 5:1). Let us take a look at the steps that make us more transparent before God.

First, we need to accept that our relationship with God is damaged. Before we can desire to restore our fellowship with God, we need to come to terms with our brokenness. God desires to be in an intimate friendship with us, but we need to know that he desires this healthy spiritual friendship. This means that we have to remove the barrier (our shame) created by our brokenness before entering into his presence. Returning to fellowship with God is our ultimate goal, and it is the place in which we find unconditional acceptance and peace. After all, we were created for the purpose to be in communion with the Almighty. Until we accept the fact that God's acceptance is not the issue, we will struggle getting closer to him. The real issue that needs to be resolved is our acceptance of him.

Second, we need to recognize that our present condition (desperately wanting to be in fellowship with God and hiding at the same time) is not what God intended for us. We were alienated from God, living in a spiritual contradiction between our original purpose and what we have become. We are saved, but with a sinful nature that continues to oppose the life of the Spirit (Rom. 7). People suffer spiritual and emotional deterioration when they continue to hide from God, even though there is no place to hide. Our goal is to regain enough trust in God to come to him for forgiveness when we fall away. Failure to grow in our intimacy with God leads to a dissatisfied life.

Nietzsche, the nineteenth century secularist, declared that God was dead. The humanistic philosophies of the twentieth century proclaimed that man had conquered the need for God. Unfortunately, the church adopted some of those worldly and dead philosophies, and we have slowly become our own gods—which was the serpent's lie to Adam and Eve in the Garden. Even with the humanistic triumphalism regarding man's psychological progress, the twentieth century was the most brutal and vicious century known to man. The church did not react with enough force against this violence. On the contrary, large segments of the church joined the socialist and communist movements of the twentieth century and ignored the persistent persecution of the church by communist dictators. These violent movements include the liberation theologies that have sprung up all over the world.

The so-called social gospel was a religious disguise for a humanistic philosophy that emptied the churches. We are seeing how the European church is hemorrhaging members, and the entire continent is moving away from the Judeo-Christian tradition that is responsible for most of its social, moral, and legal success. This destructive force that teaches that man has become his own god continues to this day. Anthony Freeman, and Anglican priest in the Church of England declared himself an atheist until he was excommunicated on August 1, 1994. An Episcopalian female priest from Rhode Island, Rev. Ann Holmes Redding, converted to Islam and she wanted to keep her parish to continue serving as a priest in a Christian organization. CNN.com reported that the Episcopal Church finally excommunicated her on Wednesday April 2, 2009. Without God, people cannot live in peace with themselves. People will search for anything, as long as it is not the true God. The solution to humanity's problems cannot be found in rejecting God, or in making a god of mortal men. G.K. Chesterton said that "when man ceases to worship God he does not worship nothing, he will worship everything."[24]

Third, we need to confront our rebellion against God through confession and repentance. These are the two elements that bring destructive secrets to light. With confession, the person comes to terms with his wrongdoing. This means that people cannot fix what is

---

[24] G. K. Chesterton. The American Chesterton Society. https://www. chesterton.org/ceases-to-worship/

wrong until they recognize whatever it is that is wrong. Repentance is the act of turning around. When people acknowledge they are headed in the wrong direction, (trying to escape, or trying to hide from God), they have the option of reversing directions. Repentance is the act of changing directions.

I believe these three steps can facilitate the restoration process to fellowship with God. We are not trying to satisfy God's demand for righteousness. God's demand for righteousness was already satisfied at the cross in Jesus. These steps are designed to allow us to approach God with confidence. He has already approached us in Christ. In the next couple of paragraphs, I want to make a brief statement about false guilt. While similar to shame, I think there are a couple of differences I would like to highlight.

Second: False Guilt

Similar to the legitimate feelings of shame, a proper response to guilt can have a healthy effect that allows people to take responsibility for wrongdoing that can lead to repentance and reconciliation with God and with others. Unlike false shame that takes place when the person's dignity is violated, false guilt appears when people believe they could have done something to prevent the spiritual injury but didn't. False guilt in its most simple expression is blaming oneself, or feeling responsible, for someone else's behavior. It creates the sensation of emotional stuck-ness. The person may have a healthy view of self but blames himself for the spiritual injury. The pain caused by the trauma is perpetuated by the false guilt that has turned internalized the blame. This inward introjection makes people reactive to their own thoughts and feelings. One major difference between false shame and false guilt is their source. False shame is the product of accepting the worthlessness of others, while false guilt is taking ownership for some else's behavior.

Also, false guilt hinders reconciliation with God and others because it is the result of accepting blame for someone else's actions. No one can repent for the actions of another. False guilt is itself an irreconcilable contradiction because it is based on a false sense of wrongdoing. Legalistic religious systems are notorious for creating false guilt. A good friend of mine was experiencing strong feelings of guilt because she was not able to get up at 4:00 am every morning to pray. She had heard that God was not pleased with us if we did not pray early in the morning, and somehow, she internalized that teaching. Since she is not a *morning person*, she carried that guilt for years. During that entire time, she felt that God was displeased with her and he was not hearing her prayers. When she shared her struggle with me, I asked her: What time does God get up in the mornings? She was stunned by my question, but laughing she said that God does not sleep. Then, I said to her: If God does not sleep and he does not care what time of the day it is, what difference does it make to him when you pray? It was incredible to see her face. A heavy weight had been removed from her soul, and she could smile again. While we need to reconcile the contradictions the trauma created, we cannot reconcile a contradiction that is based on a lie.

The most significant difference between false shame and false guilt is that the former damages *God's image* in us (our self-worth), while the latter damages our perception of *God's acceptance* of us. With false shame, we feel *unworthy* of being loved because we feel dirty. With false guilt, we feel *ineligible* to receive forgiveness because we are not valuable. That is, we reach the conclusion that our behavior is beyond God's capacity to forgive, which is a fairly arrogant statement because God has said that in Jesus he forgave all the sins of all people. Since God's capacity to forgive is limitless, the belief that we can be outside his forgiveness is clearly a lie.

Finally, like false shame, false guilt is always the result of a lie. Sometimes false guilt is the result of accepting a false belief. Other times, it is the result of a perpetrator transferring his guilt to his victim. Still others reach a false conclusion by creating a cause-and-effect connection between their suffering and their circumstances. The only way to fix a lie is with the truth that God's eternal goodness is greater than all my sins. God's grace is more than enough to fulfill his promise to forgive all who come to Jesus. The healing process for people suffering from false guilt tends to be erratic, at best. When people believe a lie, they cannot experience restoration to spiritual health until the lie is replaced with God's revealed truth.

Third: Loss of Trust

There are two basic indicators that our intimacy mechanism has suffered damage. One finds expression outside of us. The other finds expression inside of us.

First, people with a damaged intimacy mechanism have lost trust in God, and by extension, they have also lost trust in people. The dictionary defines trust as: "reliance on the integrity, strength, ability, surety, of a person or thing." If nothing is done to heal the consequences of a catastrophic spiritual injury, the individual's ability to develop healthy intimate relationships will be greatly impaired. Trust is the building block for all relationships. Without trust, people are unwilling to share their dreams and fears with others. Trust is also the essential element that makes transparency possible. It is very difficult for people to entrust their hurts to others, if they don't believe people have their best interests in mind.

Losing trust is the first casualty of a relational catastrophic spiritual injury. The answer is simple, but the reasons are not. Trust allows individuals to live without fear in their social environment. When children feel secure, for instance, they are able to face the world around them with confidence. People's childlike trust in others begins to disappear with the realization that the others can be cruel and violent. Children begin to make the connection that others cause them pain because they are selfish and uncaring. Conversely, children will reason that selfish and uncaring people are not deserving of their trust. If the people mostly responsible for their care end up hurting them, undoubtedly, they will not be able to trust those whom they do not even know. Eventually, spiritually injured people may develop a sarcastic attitude about people in general. One thing becomes clear to them—people do not deserve to enter into their sacred sanctuary of pain.

Jesus was probably thinking about this childlike trust when he stated, "I tell you the truth, unless you change and become like little children, you will never enter the kingdom of heaven. Therefore, whoever humbles himself like this child is the greatest in the kingdom of heaven" (Matt. 18:3-4). Jesus knew that children instinctively trust people. I imagine Jesus knew that, without trust, we cannot have healthy and transparent relationships. When the contradiction is detected on its initial stages (usually after the victimization has stopped), the loss of trust can be minimized. The opposite is also true; the longer the trauma is prolonged and the deeper the wound becomes, the more severe the loss of trust becomes.

Trust can also be lost when a series of minor incidents leave negative impressions on the intimacy mechanism. For example, let's say that a father promises his son to play catch with him after work. The son waits, but the father does not show up. This minor event could leave the memory of a broken promise, but it is not big enough violation to become a permanent loss of trust. If the next day the father plays catch with his son, he will not have a reason to lose trust on his father's promises. The fact that the father fixed the broken promise as soon as he had the first opportunity, in all likelihood, prevented a permanent loss of trust. However, if the broken promises become a habit, the child could lose hope and become skeptical about his father's promises. As a result of the father's failures, the intensity with which the child experiences the failed promises could influence his skepticism in trusting other people. The child may decide that if his father is not trustworthy, he does not have any reasons to trust anyone else. The child will have the tendency to project his lack of trust created by his father's failures onto society at large. Eventually, the child could accept the lie that people as a whole are not trustworthy.

Trust can be lost gradually, with a series of disappointments (superficial injuries) or it can be lost quickly when the individual suffers a violent and sudden event or the repetition of the violent event (catastrophic injuries).

Some spiritual injuries may require more intense intervention than others. Regardless of the intensity of the trauma, individuals that have suffered through them can benefit from the support of a loving community (a church) to reestablish the necessary trust in others, which is something they need to heal. Many people have overcome very serious injuries on their own, but not without a price. After years of failure and pain, all wounds begin to heal, but in many cases, this could take a lifetime. We need to offer intervention as early as possible to minimize the lasting effects spiritual injuries inflict on people's intimacy mechanism.

A damaged intimacy mechanism has an additional negative effect on trust. Some people may become overly needy because they need acceptance. This attitude can be identified when these individuals, indiscriminately share sensitive information about themselves even with complete strangers. Becoming overly needy is as dangerous as losing total trust. These individuals could over-expose themselves, becoming susceptible to more betrayals and manipulation by people that are not trustworthy. This over-exposure is an almost irresistible impulse to share every intimate detail about their lives with everybody they meet without being judiciously restrained.

This compulsive openness may appear to be a form of transparency, but in reality, is a façade that shields these individuals from actually becoming intimate. Their over-exposure has the opposite effect of what they desire because it scares other people away. Additionally, their overexposure drains other people. Most people do not know how to engage this type of unrestricted openness because the injuries serve as an impenetrable wall of separation. The overexposed people do not know how to get close to others without overwhelming them with their issues. As a result, they will have the tendency to overestimate the value of telling everything to everyone. This overly trusting attitude is a cry for empathy that endangers the person to further rejection from unscrupulous individuals who can take advantage of their uncontrollable need for acceptance and intimacy at all costs. The overexposed person's intense need for acceptance makes them targets for manipulation. In either case, the person needs to be restored to a balanced trusting perspective in order for transparency to be a sincere and an effective effort to connect with God and with others.

We have already established that without trust it is very difficult to develop transparency with God and other people. Becoming transparent with God is a good indicator that trust has been restored. John stated that confession is the most effective way to demonstrate transparency. Hear his words: "If we confess our sins, he is faithful and just and will forgive us our sins and purify us from all unrighteousness" (1 Jn. 1:9). The apostle's point was that when we confess we are opening ourselves to God. The second part of the text is also encouraging. After confession, God will forgive, and we will feel accepted. If lack of transparency signals that trust is missing, then, trusting means that we are sufficiently transparent to develop healthy intimate relationships.

Trust is an attitude in the individuals' psyche that influences their decision-making process. That is, people need to know that not everything is a conspiracy against them. They can actually enjoy the rain without thinking that God just wanted to ruin their new suit. A loss of trust in people eventually turns into a loss of trust in God and vice-versa. It does not matter which one comes first. The one will lead to the other. Since the loss of trust is the result of a spiritual injury that damages the intimacy mechanism, it really does not matter if we lose trust in God or people first. Regardless of its initial target, God or people, the loss of trust often extends to other areas of our lives. The obvious conclusion is that if people believe God is the cause of their suffering, then, they would not have any reasons to trust him. The spiritually injured person does not realize that this kind of thinking is based on a lie.

One of the basic assumptions in this book is that God created us to establish reciprocal healthy and spiritual relationships with him. Thus, a properly functioning intimacy mechanism recognizes that our ability to love is a gift from God. This understanding is paramount to our spiritual health. Loving God and neighbor is God's purpose for our lives, and it is God's method to assist us in finding fulfillment. We need to remember that our lostness from God's presence is defined as broken fellowship with God. On this subject, Paul told the Ephesian church that we "were dead in our trespasses and sins" (Eph. 2:1). That is, a broken fellowship from God has the same impact of being dead. Imagine that! Being isolated and rejected is as bad as being dead. The apostle Paul also added that when we "were dead in [our] sins and in the un-circumcision of [our] sinful nature, God made [us] alive with Christ. He forgave us all our sins (Col. 2:13-14). Salvation is both, freedom from the penalty of eternal death, and restoration to fellowship with God through "reconciliation" (Rom. 5:10).

Therefore, we can't find fulfillment for our lives if we are alienated from God and neighbor. God's love in us compels us to share love with others. We need to understand that Jesus's teaching about the two great commandments in the parable of the Good Samaritan were not given to castigate the religious leaders of the day (Lk. 10:25-37). They knew those commandments very well. The commandments were given as indicators that we cannot find fulfillment in religious fanaticism or adherence to the Law. The ultimate fulfillment for our lives is found in loving our neighbors as evidence that God's grace is flowing through us. The two great commandments (to love God and to love neighbor) fill the most profound and essential need in the human soul – to live a reconciled relationship with God and in fellowship with one another. It should not be surprising that Jesus declared that these two commandments captured the meaning and the spirit of the entire Law and the prophets. If we want to enjoy God's purpose for our lives, we must become a neighbor to those in need while being reconciled with God.

The second issue people experience with a damaged intimacy mechanism is a distorted perception of self (of God's image in us). This is similar to the distortion caused by false shame, but it is different in one major respect. The loss of trust is not always the result of a violent spiritual injury, such as sexual or physical abuse. For example, when two people go through a divorce, they could be sending at least two messages to one another. The person seeking divorce says, "I can do better without you because you cannot make me happy." The person who does not want the divorce says, "Apparently, I am not good enough for you. If I were, you would not leave me." Both statements damage the self-esteem of the partner committed to saving the marriage.

If people come to believe they are not good enough to be in an intimate relationship with someone else, they can spend much of their lives trying to prove themselves to others. People with low self-esteem believe that any rejection is a poor reflection of who they are as individuals. They could develop the tendency to internalize those rejections as evidence that they are flawed and damaged. If anything goes wrong, it is their fault. If something goes right, it could not have been their doing. After all, they can't do anything worthy of praise. If they cannot solve personal problems, it's because they are weak or dumb. They make generalizations like: "people hate me" or "since

God does not care about me I make the best of a bad situation and survive the best way I know how." For these individuals, survival becomes the only goal, but survival comes with a price. They have a terrible sadness and loneliness that robs them of their joy.

In order to survive, they will use every defense mechanism available to them, from becoming sarcastic to being skeptical about people's motives. In some instances, their skepticism could lead to the loss of faith in God. The way they see it, God certainly did not do anything to remedy their situation, and he should not expect devotion and faithfulness from them. But there is a remedy, which is as old as God himself. Since God created us to be in fellowship with him, our ability to recognize this truth will open the door for acceptance and the rediscovery of our intrinsic worth with which God created us. This discovery is the key to transforming our outlook in life. It begins with accepting God's goodness.

Allow me to share a word of caution. Secrets are not necessarily evil. However, when the secrets are hiding crippling spiritual injuries, as described by Maria, they could poison the spiritual health of the family unit. Not all spiritual injuries result in family secrets. For example, divorces cause spiritual injuries in all the parties involved, but they have the tendency to be very public events. However, even though most divorces are very public events, the conditions that caused them may not be.

If a secret covers up a violent dysfunction within the family unit, the cost of keeping the secret could be the destruction of the family itself. In other words, the secret that was kept hidden to protect the family becomes the very thing that destroys it. In Maria's example, failure to address the grandfather's shameless and predatory behavior resulted in emotional and spiritual harm to three generations of girls in that family. We do not even know how each girl in that family struggled to maintain their self-worth, their dignity, their false sense of shame, or even how the daughters became enablers that allowed the grandfather to attack their own daughters.

A proper interpretation of God's Word leads to the conclusion that our relationship with God cannot be restored without transparency. We can define transparency as people's ability to confess their sins to God and to make restitution to the people they have sinned against. Adam and Eve provided the primary example of how lack of transparency causes irreparable damage to our relationship with God. On the one hand, Adam and Eve's behavior represented a desperate attempt to hide their shame from God. On the other hand, David is the primary example of a man that chose to confront his shame recognizing that he could not escape God's omniscience. We will benefit greatly to follow David's example and learn to live in God's presence.

We began this chapter stating that catastrophic spiritual injuries have three distinct symptoms: (1) false shame, (2) false guilt, and (3) loss of trust. In order to get people past these three destructive consequences, we need to identify the circumstances that give them legitimacy as well as the instinctive reactiveness that is used to cover up the pain caused by the original spiritual injury. The healing process improves dramatically when; (1) we recognize the lies we have believed for a long time, and (2) when we reject the power of the lies to condition our responses to circumstances. Eventually, people who have been injured by relational traumas have to move away from the lies to make healing a real possibility. Otherwise, they could waste valuable time and effort managing the ghosts of false guilt, false shame, and loss of trust.

CHAPTER 5

Transparency: Learning to Trust Again

Amanda was nineteen when I first met her. She was wearing a baseball hat so low over her face that I could barely see her chin. Immediately, I concluded that she was hiding a tremendous amount of shame. I thought that her healing would become visible when I could see her eyes. She told me that her family was very secretive. There were certain topics they simply did not talk about in the house. This was especially true about anything related to sexuality. No one was allowed to mention those subjects during dinner table conversation.

Amanda was the second child of five (two boys and three girls). She was the oldest girl. When she turned eight, her father came to her bed one night and stayed with her. She found her father's actions strange, but he was her father, and since he did not do anything that day, she did not say anything. A few days later her father returned to her bed, and on this occasion, he made physical contact with her. She moved his hands away, but he told her that it was customary for fathers to sleep with their daughters and that her mom was in agreement with his actions. At that moment, Amanda told me that she felt trapped. She guessed she had to submit to her father's advances. She did not feel she could object, even though she found her father's actions repugnant. After that day, her father's visits became a weekly event. He moved from touching her for a couple of years, to actual intercourse when she turned ten. He used her sexually until she was fifteen. Amanda was a brilliant student and she dedicated herself to study and graduated from high school at sixteen. As soon as she graduated, she moved away from home and thought that all was well.

However, on one of her visits back home, about two years later, she suspected that something had been happening to her youngest sister, who was six years younger, and who was now twelve years old. After Amanda insisted for a few minutes, her sister told her that her father had been molesting her since she was eight. This meant that their father had moved to the two younger sisters while Amanda was still living in the house. Amanda's second sister was now fifteen and her father was no longer interested in her, but he had sexually abused her in the same way he had done to Amanda. None of the sisters knew that their father had started his predatory behavior with all of them shortly after their eighth birthdays. When Amanda came home on that occasion, she knew her younger sister had been a victim for at least four years. Amanda asked me what she should do.

I told her that the first order of business was to get her two sisters out or the house. I encouraged her to tell her mother, or to confront her if she was complicit with her father. Initially, she did not what to do it, but she finally realized she needed to get her two sisters out of that house. Now as an adult, she could bring them with her away from their father. She decided to confront her mother about taking the sisters out of the house. When the mother heard her story, she went ballistic. She became hysterical and went to school to bring the two girls home from school. She asked the girls, and they too confirmed Amanda's story. Amanda's mother called the cops and cried the entire time because she claimed she did not know what had been happening. She believed her husband was sleeping outside their bedroom because he had some type of sexual dysfunction or was having an affair, but she told Amanda that she never suspected what he had been doing for years. The mother believed her daughters, but she could not understand how her husband of twenty-two years could have done this to his own daughters. The father was arrested that day, and after the trial he was sentenced to twenty-five years in prison.

Amanda was broken, but she was able to get her two sisters out, but unfortunately not before they too had been exposed to their predator father. Curiously, Amanda was in my office because she felt shamed by her father's actions, and even though she continued to excel in school, she had not been able to get rid of the shame. We met several times before the first rays of light started to appear. Several months after the entire episode had unraveled, Amanda stopped by the office with her customary hat, but on this time, I saw her eyes for the first time. She told me that she was very grateful and that she was ready to move on. I told her that I believed she was ready, but that she could come back if she needed to talk. I saw Amanda one more time, and on this occasion, she was not wearing her customary hat. That day we joked about school, and I knew she was ready. I pray that Amanda realized her dream to become a doctor, and that her sisters are doing as well as I believe she is. Amanda's courage defanged the secret, and with her actions she rescued her two sisters from the brutality of their own father.

The Antidote for Secrets

A definition for transparency would be helpful to guide our remaining discussion on this subject.

> Transparency – is exhibiting openness, accountability, and candor in our relationship with God. True transparency proceeds from repentance and eliminates the false sense of shame or the constant fear of retribution. It is to stand "naked" before God without the urge to hide our sins from his presence. Trusting in God's grace opens the gate for sincere transparency.

This definition forms the basis for our discussion in this chapter. We need a clear understanding of God's requirement for transparency in order to achieve the desired spiritual health. God hated Adam's and Eve's feeble attempts to hide from him. He despises the darkness of secrecy because it is nothing more than an illusion of protection against God's piercing eyes. We deceive ourselves when we believe we can hide from God. It is this self-deception that sends us into a hide-and-seek game with God that breaks down our relationship with him. God's deepest desire is our friendship. True friendship requires honest and sincere personal interaction. Transparency (openness) opens the door and encourages trust. Trust is present when people are willing to risk putting their well-being on someone else's hands without questioning the other person's motives because they believe their motives are good for them. Trust, in turn, encourages people to become emotionally closer, or to become more intimate, to their object of trust. Therefore, if people are emotionally distant or closed, they are unable to trust others which in turn prevents them from being transparent in their relationships.

Said in another way, trust is the external expression of the inner confidence that we have been accepted. And feeling accepted is the foundation for transparency. We cannot become vulnerable to someone that does not have our best interests in mind. This is one of the reasons we are not transparent with people we do not know. We almost never know how much they have accepted us the way we are. Spiritual health is simply not possible without transparency. A lack of transparency enables feelings of shame to send us running for cover (literally and figuratively), as Adam did when he said, "I was afraid because I was naked; so, I hid" (Gen. 3:10). The above definition of transparency has three basic elements and two conditions.

First, openness is a reference to a person's decision to become vulnerable to another by trusting their needs and trials to them. Openness means that people take down the well-constructed walls that prevent people from having access into their lives. Openness, therefore, is a reference to access. When people are emotionally and spiritually open to others, they can be engaged in an intimate relationship without the fear that their spiritual struggles will be dismissed or mocked.

Second, accountability is a reference to the fact that we do not function or exist in a social vacuum. This aspect of transparency is a little more complicated because accountability goes beyond allowing access to others. To be accountable to another person means the willingness to have a different party to check upon one's behavior before they vouch for our character. Accountability requires the type of humility that allows people to submit to someone else's instruction and discipline. When people become accountable they add an external source of power that strengthens their resolve to overcome temptation. Also, accountability keeps the dysfunction transparent—or exposed—and it defangs the power that it has while it was hiding in the shadows. Accountability forces the issue and provides the background for transparency that in turn could develop into trusting relationship. But it is ineffective when people are in a state of rebellion or are unwilling to allow others to enter their business.

God has always focused his attention on people's hearts. This was true as far back as when God sent the prophet Samuel to anoint a new king for Israel. When Samuel put his eyes on the man that looked best suited for the position, God told the prophet, "Do not consider his appearance or his height, for I have rejected him. The LORD does not look at the things man looks at. Man looks at the outward appearance, but the LORD looks at the heart" (1 Sam. 16:7). Jesus made a similar statement when he said, "Stop judging by mere appearances, and make a right judgment" (Jn. 7:24).

We are limited to evaluate people by superficial judgments, but God has the ability to examine people's motives and attitudes. This is the reason Jesus declared that the poor widow gave more than all the rich men combined. How can a fraction of a penny be worth more than the rest of the money? (Mk. 12:41-44). The reason is that God does not measure our lives based on what we can do or give. God evaluates the attitudes and motives of the heart because he relates to us through the heart. He does not need anything from us. It is a waste of time to try to impress him with our actions. The poor widow did not try. She simply gave her heart to God.

God recognized Adam's and Eve's rebellion for what it was, a crude attempt to set themselves up as gods. After all, that was what the serpent promised them. "For God knows that when you eat of it your eyes will be opened, and you will be like God..." (Gen. 3:5). God was not interested in their physical location. He wanted them to answer why they had chosen to forsake their transparency. Their hiding was the external indicator that something had gone wrong in their spiritual relationship with God. This pattern is still true today. People tend to have physical responses to the sins of the heart. This is the reason the Bible states that, "from the abundance of the heart the mouth will speak" (Lk. 6:45). To this day people have not overcome the impulse to hide from God when they sin.

Third, transparency demands candor. A person's willingness to live by the truth is a testimony that they have nothing to hide. Lack of candor is best seen when excuses and lies are the initial response to any situation. People lie as a compulsion to conceal their real self, whether is something they have done or something they want to avoid doing. When Cain killed his brother Abel (Gen. 4:1-15), God asked Cain to tell him the truth about the event that took Abel's life. Cain's response was a very defensive question that did not answer God's question, but that affirmed an eternal principle. Cain asked God, "Am I my brother's keeper?" The answer to Cain's question was implied in the question. His instinctive reaction was to deny that he had been with Abel. Did he not realize that he could not hide from God's presence?

The answer to the question is very simple. Yes, Cain, you are your brother's keeper, but you killed him in a jealous rage. Cain's initial response to God was to hide the truth. When Cain answered God with his evasive question, he did not technically lie. He was trying to avoid the truth. At some point in their life's journey, people have to realize they cannot hide anything from God. He knows our words before they form in our minds. In addition to the three elements of transparency, openness, accountability and candor, there are two pre-conditions for transparency.

Preconditions for Transparency

First, before transparency is even possible, people have to be willing to accept their brokenness when confronted with it or when the Holy Spirit of God moves within their consciences. That is, denial of sin, wrongdoing, or brokenness, is an indicator that people lack the will to be transparent. Men and women have been trying for centuries to device philosophies that excuse their sins. Even today, we have twisted our language to avoid confronting anything that might come close to sin. People prefer to feel good about their sins, and to avoid confronting it as long as they can.

Second, we need to reestablish the proper perspective in our relationship with God—he is the creator and we are the created. Satan's temptation to Adam and Eve was, ultimately, about worship. When Satan told the first couple that if they ate of the "tree of the knowledge of good and evil" they would become like God, he was awaking in Adam and Eve the desire for adoration, admiration, and worship. It is in this area, more than any other, that our perspective in our relationship with God is properly established. The first three commandments are intended to reestablish the proper alignment between God and us. They read thus,

> "You shall have no other gods before me. You shall not make for yourself an idol in the form of anything in heaven above or on the earth beneath or in the waters below. You shall not bow down to them or worship them…" (Ex. 20:3-5)

There are no other gods in heaven or on earth. The serpent wanted Adam and Eve to focus on their present physical reality. The devil continues the same tactic to this day. Basically, the devil wants people to focus on their present physical pleasures and conditions. If he succeeds in this endeavor, people will be as deceived as Adam and Eve were. This is the reason the Bible states that Satan lied from the beginning. He is still lying to this day. No one on earth or heaven is worthy of worship except God. When we enter God's presence with a worshipful attitude we acknowledge both the Creator's position as God and our position as not being God.

Slippery Slope of Temptation

A sinful heart does not develop overnight. I have identified three steps that lead to sin. First, we are faced with a temptation disguised as a legitimate choice between two or more options of equal value. James tells us that temptations are the result of our inner sinful instincts. He stated that,

> "Each one is tempted when, by his own evil desire, he is dragged away and enticed. Then, after desire has conceived, it gives birth to sin; and sin, when it is full-grown, gives birth to death" (Jam. 1:14-15).

Second, the temptation becomes a real alternative. When our desires are not aligned with God's character, the option to surrender to the temptation is birthed from within. Our desires, misguided by our sinful nature, lead us to the path of rebellion against God. Let us note that sin is basically a behavior that runs counter to God's intended design and purpose for us.

Third, after the sin has been consummated, we deceive ourselves into believing we can escape God's presence. The story of the rich young ruler illustrates this point (Lk. 18:18-22). The rich young ruler came to Jesus and asked, "Good teacher, what must I do to inherit eternal life?" He believed he was on solid ground. He was convinced he had kept all the commandments and there was not much more that God could require of him. In other words, the young ruler was pretty satisfied with his own righteousness.

The rich young ruler's problem, and our problem, is that Jesus looks for the hidden things in our hearts. Jesus told the young ruler (paraphrasing): "If you are sincere in your desire to inherit the kingdom of God, then you have to deal with the greed hiding behind your external expression of piety based on the law." Jesus used the following phrase to bring the rich young ruler's heart into the open: "You still lack one thing. Sell everything you have and give to the poor, and you will have treasure in heaven. Then come, follow me" (Lk. 18:22). Jesus's words must have felt like a sucker punch to the stomach. The rich young ruler's nakedness was exposed for all to see. He had deceived himself into believing that he could hide his sin of greed from God. Our feeble attempts to hide from God are nothing but a self-delusion.

Our consciences alert us immediately that we have sinned. The rich young ruler knew exactly Jesus's point—he still had too much greed, which is idolatry, in his soul to enter heaven. The level of our intimacy with God will be determined by our next step. If we come to him in humility and confess our sin seeking forgiveness, we will be restored. But if we turn away in shame and shun him, we will forever live separate from God. The Lord wants to expose our shame, so we can live in his presence totally open to him. He calls us to accountability for our benefit, not his.

Shining the Light on Destructive Secrets

The prophet came for one of his regular visits with David. Since Nathan had free access to the king, he decided to share a short real-life story with David to wrestle an emotional response from the king. "There was a rich man," he began, "who invited some people over to his house for dinner. This man owned one hundred sheep. He had a neighbor who only owned one sheep. The rich man chose to kill his neighbor's sheep to feed his guests instead of choosing one from his vast flock." "Tell me, King David," asked the prophet, "what is your opinion about that rich man?" David was beside himself. His response was predictable and harsh. The man who took the one sheep should die. The prophet calmly told the king, "You are that man." As the king of Israel, you could have taken any woman for a wife, but you chose Uriah's wife and then killed him (2 Sam. 11:1-12, 25).

David fell on his face and immediately began the process of seeking God's forgiveness. He had understood his sin. The struggle within David was so intense that he wrote in Psalm 51:1, "Have mercy on me, O God, according to your unfailing love; according to your great compassion blot out my transgressions." He then added in v. 3, "For I know my transgressions;" and v. 4, "Against you, you only, have I sinned;" and v. 10, "Create in me a pure heart;" and finally on v. 12, "Restore to me the joy of your salvation."

David's life is a perfect example of God's grace. But it is also a perfect example of what God is looking for in a man's heart. God wants transparency and accountability. These two qualities made him "a man after God's own heart" (1 Sam. 13:14). Certainly no one would think David was a model of decency. His morality was that of a scoundrel. We know he was not a good father: he did not discipline one of his sons, Amnon, who raped his own sister, Tamar. He was a failure as a husband; his wives could manipulate him with impunity; and he was not even able to remain faithful to his own family.

In spite of his many flaws and failures, David had one quality that God could not ignore. He never once denied God. He never once hid his sins from God. The second king of Israel is the classic example of a man who lives a transparent life. This character quality is fundamental to the healing process from spiritual injuries and the crippling effects of spiritual scars, blind spots, and instinctive reactive behaviors.

The ultimate goal of the healing process is to repair the intimacy mechanism. The intimacy mechanism allows people to engage God and neighbor in healthy spiritual relationships. The most visible and recognizable result of a damaged intimacy mechanism is loss of trust. Without trust, we cannot become transparent enough to engage God and neighbor, or to allow them to engage us. Without trust, we will not be able to fulfill our God-given purposes of "Loving God" and "loving neighbor." This is not to say that people cannot love at all. This is to say that without trust people's ability to risk loving others has the tendency to be guarded, insecure, and self-centered. A damaged intimacy mechanism sends a signal of fear whenever we are getting too emotionally close to other people. The purpose of the signal of fear is to back off from the possible intimate relationship.

It is a fact that people experience different levels of trust. However, when people's trust level is low, they would have the tendency to be overly cautious in their relationships. It follows that people cannot love unconditionally unless they are able to trust God and others. Actually, the lower people's trust level, the more conditional their relationships become. Learning to trust again is a key indicator that the intimacy mechanism is mending. Trust opens the door that allows us to engage God without fear in a transparent relationship.

Many people who have suffered damage to the intimacy mechanism become involved in unhealthy relationships. If the damage is the result of violence, they could assume that violence is the relational norm. If the damage was caused by neglect, their ability to show affection could become limited. If the loss of trust is defined through a sexually distorted image of self, the tendency to sexual compulsion could become uncontrollable. People's need for acceptance can rob them of the freedom to say no without thinking that they are hurting other people's feelings. Sometimes people can feel betrayed by others when their efforts are not appreciated. It is as if the only way to relate with others is to assume the victim's role.

As the reader can appreciate, we are dealing with very complicated issues that are not easily resolved. We need to approach each spiritual injury as a unique event in a person's life. This is due to the fact that each individual is unique. Even though spiritual injuries are particular to the individuals struggling with them, they are not isolated events. Additionally, they are unique because individuals will respond differently to similar traumas. This is the reason we insist that spiritual injuries leave as many different scars and blind spots as there are people. As we have also discussed, people's ability to respond to a spiritual injury is influenced by their social environment, their family upbringing, and their ability to trust others. For example, a child that had a high trust-level with a perpetrator before the injury could experience a wider congruency gap between his expected truth (this person should have protected me) and his reality (this person has intentionally damaged me). Obviously, the wider is the congruency gap, the more pronounced is the contradiction that produced the spiritual injury.

We also need to deal with the context in which the injury occurred. The context is important to determine the severity of the spiritual injury. If people are traumatized by those who should have protected them, their injuries could be experienced as much more severe than if it the trauma was caused by strangers. This is not to say that being abused by strangers is not severe. Rather, it is to say that the damage feels more vicious and violent when someone the child trusted is the cause of the injury. This is even more damaging when the family environment facilitated the injurious event. While it is necessary to identify the injury as an event in itself, we cannot ignore the context that may have facilitated its occurrence. Our focus is to pinpoint the spiritual injury, as such, without ignoring how the context could have played a role in the event that produced it.

We are in a never-ending process to find peace for our souls. This process requires that we have clarity regarding certain essential truths about God and the human condition. Transparency before God is the foundational element of the healing process. Secrecy is the opposite of transparency because it hides the injury, protects the perpetrators, and keeps the victims trapped in an emotional hell.

King David's Path to Transparency

We already spoke briefly about David. I will use Psalm 139 as my point of reference to illustrate a transparent life. David makes the following statements to address his willingness to appear naked before God.

> v. 1 – O Lord, you have searched me, and you know me.

> v. 3 – You discern my going out and my lying down.

> v. 5 – You hem me in behind and before.

> v. 7 – Where can I go from your Spirit?

> v. 11, 12 – If I say, "Surely the darkness will hide me... even the darkness will not be dark to you."

David acknowledged in v. 7 that he could not run, hide, or escape from God's presence. He concluded the psalm with a statement of openness and accountability. "Search me, O God, and know my heart; test me and know my anxious thoughts. See if there is any offensive way in me and lead me in the way everlasting" (Ps. 139: 23-24).

This is not to say that David was a sinless example of godliness. We all know David's personal issues. They are recorded in Scripture for all to see. But David was an excellent example of transparency. How do we know this? God Himself testified of David's openness. The Lord called David "a man after God's own heart" (1 Sam. 13:14).

People fall out of fellowship with God when they choose to hide their sins instead of confessing them. Since nothing sinful or evil can be in God's holy presence, any attempt to hide from God, is an indication that our fellowship with God is already broken. Confessing our sins means that we don't want to hide from God. This transparency means that we desire intimacy with God.

Restoring the Intimacy Mechanism

Relational spiritual injuries are like a crippling virus that attacks the host's intimacy mechanism. Every time the intimacy mechanism is severely damaged, people's ability to develop healthy relationships with God, self, and others is greatly diminished. God created us to live in community. This is the reason we do not do well in isolation. Actually, the Bible said from the beginning that "it is not good for man to be alone" (Gen. 2:18). God designed us to be engaged in healthy emotional relationships with God and with others. The basis for these relationships is a healthy perception of self in relationship to God. Thus, Jesus stated that we needed "to love our neighbor as we love ourselves." He was not talking about a selfish narcissistic self-love. He was revealing the simple fact that we can only give to others what we have. If we do not have love, we cannot give love. Therefore, a healthy perception of our own worth and dignity makes it possible for us to extend that to others.

In this context, trust should not be understood as a blind following. Rather, trust is the natural belief that people are generally reliable and honorable. This is not a reference to the theological concept that we are all sinners and need repentance to be in fellowship with God. I am simply stating that people, as a whole, do not wake up every single day with a desire to harm others and curse God. Therefore, I have concluded that most people want the same things, peace of mind, a little bit of happiness, and a decent job to pay for their personal and family needs. Are there evil people who wake up with the desire to harm others? Of course. But I believe this a minority group.

The most serious injuries are directly connected to the injured people's inability to relate with their environment without spiritual anxiety and fear. I have heard countless people say, "I've always had trust issues." They know the problem. They cannot trust others. They know that their lack of trust is a hindrance to healthy intimate relationships. They, however, do not know how they lost their ability to trust, or how to regain it. People find themselves alienated from others and God because of an intense fear of engaging in transparent intimacy.

Spiritual wounds are not always recognized as such, especially when they occurred in childhood. Children do not have the emotional and experiential capacity to recognize the nature of the injury or defend themselves from predators or abusive adults. They are vulnerable to suffer spiritual injuries in which they did not play an active role. This is especially true in the case of sex abuse and physical violence. In most instances, people remember the trauma, but they are not always able to recognize the lasting effects it left on the intimacy mechanism. They remember the suffering and the abuse, but they would rather forget the entire event than to relive it.

Relational injuries occur too often, but we should not ignore the more common spiritual injuries that cover a wide range of situations such as: experiencing the parent's divorce, a rejection from group participation in a school play or sports, feeling abandoned by parents who are too busy making a living, etc. As we have mentioned earlier, self-medication is the most common response to a persistent but unrecognized spiritual pain. Addictions provide a viable but superficial alternative way to manage the uncontrollable and persistent restlessness. Most people do not want to engage in self-destructive behaviors, and yet many end up craving a drink, a snort, a smoke or even suicide.

A good way to answer the above question is with an illustration. In the movie 50 First Dates[25] a young woman was involved in an accident, and she lost all her short-term memory. The family decided to arrange her life circumstances so that she would relive the same day over and over. Regardless of what she experienced in her new day, everything was as if she had lived the day of the accident. If the family had not intervened and created an alternate reality to relive the same day over and over, she could have lost her connection to her known reality. She experienced her days as if the accident had never happened. Her father and brother had to ensure that the newspaper, her trip, her vehicle, and even her attire was exactly as she remembered them the day of the accident. Like all fantasies, everything began to change when a young man fell in love with her. She began to experience new things, but could not remember her

---

[25]   First 50 Dates.

dates with the man. It was as if they had never met. There was a blind spot in her consciousness that she was not able to overcome.

The people who engage in self-destructive behaviors, and as a result end up self-medicating, lose control over their desires and feelings. Their reactions are instinctive and subconscious. They may even make promises to themselves and their families that they will change. They say they will never again engage in the behavior. While they mean well, and they actually desire to stop the self-inflicted damage, they cannot make the adjustment. In the movie, Adam Sandler (the boyfriend) came up with the idea of taping her days to show her how they had met, etc. Every morning she would watch the video and she could then live her day remembering her new boyfriend. In essence, the daily video of her past gave her a sense of direction and accountability to deal with her blind spot. Accountability is an integral aspect of protection against the relational vacuum created by the damaged intimacy mechanism. Until people realize that blind spots exist and that they block their ability to make the necessary adjustments, the compulsive behaviors will remain.

We can ascertain the severity of the damage the spiritual injury might have caused to the intimacy mechanism by people's difficulties in establishing emotionally healthy relationships with God and others. Injured people could become obsessed with the need to ease their pain through any means necessary. They will spend most of their waking hours thinking of the next peaceful moment or their next fix. They constantly ask, "When can I rest from this pain?" Since the restlessness does not go away, they become driven to look for emotionally charged experiences to distract from the pain. As soon as the injured individuals achieve the much-desired relief, the search for the next moment of temporal relief begins. There is no time to waste. The ever-present fear that relief will elude them is too much to consider. They need to go to the club again, or they need two more beers, or they need to find their next sexual encounter. And they have to do it fast because reflection and aloneness are not desirable options.

The obsession to eliminate the pain turns into an emotional hell. The drive towards finding relief is the only thing that matters. People who have experienced catastrophic spiritual injuries have one common pitfall. Compulsive or self-destructive behaviors drive them. But there is hope. There is a way to find peace for the brokenhearted.

Intimacy with God

I think the parable of the Prodigal Son illustrates this point beautifully (Lk. 15:11-32). The prodigal son is both a metaphor for every individual who has tried to live independent of God, from Adam to this day, and an example of a life's journey away from, and back to, God. The parable describes the son of a wealthy man who wanted to make his own living independent of the father's influence and wealth. The son, who probably had not been paying attention, did not know how wealth was created. He believed he could walk away from his father's wealth without consequences. The prodigal son asked his father to give him his inheritance, so he could make his own choices and enjoy the pleasures of life.

The prodigal son left his father's house and began to enjoy parties and friends, and as long as the money lasted, he could lie to himself that life was good. As the prodigal moved further away from the father, he arrived at a place where there was a famine in the land. While Jesus was using the physical concept of hunger, he was making reference to the spiritual famine people experience when they distance themselves from their intimacy with God. When the money ran out, the prodigal son was destitute, hungry, and sharing food with pigs. In other words, he had become a dishonorable man. In a matter of a few years he went from riches to rags (the Bible does not say how long it took him to lose everything).

While in this desperate condition, when he hit rock bottom, Jesus tells us that he came to his senses. He looked up to the heavens and realized that even the servants in his father's house were better off than he was so far away from the fellowship with his father. In order to escape his rock bottom of intimacy with God, the prodigal son took three definite steps.

First, he had to acknowledge his brokenness. He did not have anything, even though he could have had everything. He was broken, even though he could be made whole. He had sunk to the depths of desperation, even though he could have had peace and plenty. He was broken, and he knew it. This is the essential first step to restore a healthy spiritual relationship—to recognize that our intimacy with the Father in Heaven is broken and needs to be repaired.

The second step to restore intimacy with the father, the prodigal had to decide to return to his father's house. He reasoned that shame and embarrassment would not prevent him from returning home. In other words, the prodigal son had to get rid of his pride. He had to humble himself and accept that his decision to abandon his father was wrongheaded. His choice to leave his father had backfired and he needed to be humble enough to recognize that his dependency on parties, women, and drugs had only brought sadness, loneliness, shame, and despair. Once the prodigal accepted his desperate state, he needed to take the third step.

Finally, the prodigal son took the courageous steps to actually return home. It is one thing to recognize when we have hit rock bottom. It's another thing to acknowledge how we got there. But it's even more courageous to take the steps towards spiritual health and restoration to intimacy. He did not return home making any demands. He came looking for mercy and grace. The father, who had always loved his son, recognized him in the distance. He ran to him and welcomed him back because this "son was dead, but he was alive again."

People need to understand the Father is ready to restore them to intimacy with him. Some people are on their way to rock bottom, some have already hit rock bottom, but God is still waiting to restore them to a better life with him. To return to God we have to acknowledge our brokenness and renounce our pride. It takes courage to do those two things. In this context, courage is always the result of a fundamental belief that one's actions are required to resolve whatever problem we are facing. Soldiers show courage in the line of fire when they accept the obligation to take an action to defend others' well-being, even if they have to risk their own lives. But we need a totally different type of courage to recognize one's own failure, get rid of personal pride, and humble one-self in someone else's presence. But, if injured people want to escape rock bottom, this courage is absolutely necessary. People will realize that spiritual blindness and pride are the two primary obstacles that prevent those who are at rock bottom to seek restoration to intimacy, which is the solution to the brokenness they have experienced in their lives.

Intimacy with Neighbor

Jesus left us two commandments: "love God with all your heart, with all your mind, and with all your soul", and "love your neighbor as yourself" (Lk. 10:27). Jesus did not give these two commandments to compliment the old Ten Commandments. He gave them to replace the old law, which was designed to regulate behavior. But Jesus established the two new commandments as a new law that regulates the heart. Jesus's purpose was to bring peace and rest to the brokenhearted. He promised that if we come to him, he would give us rest (Matt. 11:28). In order for us to need rest, we must be restless. Jesus's message was that as long as people are separated from God, they cannot find the rest they most desire. But he also wanted to make sure people understood that peace with God was only one side of the equation. We also need to be restored to fellowship with others.

All of us have experienced spiritual injuries to one degree or another. However, no two people will respond to similar spiritual injuries in the same way. Thus, while we consider our injuries to be serious and deep, we may consider someone else's suffering to be superficial and insignificant. Some of us could even become judgmental and say that other people exaggerate their suffering and pain.

The proverbial saying of "putting ourselves in someone else's shoes" sounds romantic, but in practice it is very difficult to do, unless we can identify ourselves with the specific injuries of others. In order to put ourselves in someone else's shoes, we need to develop the type of empathy that is the result of our own suffering. When we see someone suffering a similar injury, we have the tendency to *connect* with that person much easier. However, when the other person is suffering from an injury we do not share, we could become more callous and less accessible to "put ourselves in their shoes."

If we take a survey around us, we can find that many social workers, nurses, doctors, and even lawyers, choose those professions because they have a deep sense of empathy with people as a result of a deeply felt spiritual injury. This is not true in every case, but we can find many stories in which it is.

I met a lawyer who chose the legal profession because his father spent time in jail for a crime he did not commit. The father's incarceration was short, but the son decided that he would become a lawyer to defend people who are wrongfully accused. This young man's father went through a painful trial, and after spending seven months in jail, the real culprit of the crime was caught committing a different crime. The police were able to connect him to the crime for which the young man's father was in jail. Even after the real criminal was captured, it took another six months before the courts decided to let the man free. It is not difficult to see how a son would want to become a lawyer after such a painful memory.

CHAPTER 6

Trusting: Learning to Love Again

The following are several initial steps people can take in their spiritual healing process. First, individuals need to accept that the self-destructive behavior exists and that if they continue to engage in self-medication, it will destroy their ability to relate with the world around them and eventually it will kill them. Second, people need to accept that the reason for their dysfunctional behaviors is the need to hide their shame, low self-esteem, or desire to fit in, etc. Third, they need to identify the source of their pain. This step requires that they identify the events and the players responsible for their spiritual injuries. Fourth, individuals need to connect their pain to a specific traumatic event that resulted in an irreconcilable contradiction. Fifth, they need to accept that a spiritual injury has produced blind spots, they have believed a lie, and have become overly reactive as a result. Sixth, spiritually injured individuals need to accept that these blind spots cannot be erased, but they can be neutralized. Blind spots can be identified in at least three ways: (1) when there is a feeling that others are pushing their hot buttons; (2) when there is a pattern of failure in the same type of temptations; and (3) when there is a pattern of instinctive reactivity to people and situations.

Many people express suicidal thoughts as a result of their anger towards their inability to escape the vicious cycle of dependency. They cannot see options or exit doors for their present predicament. Others suffer from terrible personal disappointments and have lost the will to survive their present condition. They could feel hopeless because the cure for their spiritual injuries have become elusive or because they cannot rid themselves of the feelings of shame. Spiritually injured people find it more desirable to experience the constant frenzy of their dysfunctions than to do any self-reflection on the unbearable spiritual pain they experience, even if the dysfunctions cost them their happiness, their families, and their lives.

Mark was thirty-two years old man who had been married and divorced three times and had failed at six other relationships. He was always lonely, but he could never find the right partner to make a life together. His brokenness was deep and painful. Mark was trapped. He desired normalcy in his life. He wanted a family, with kids, and a good woman whom he could trust. But that was the problem. Mark could not trust women. In his desperate attempt to gain control, he had lost control by turning to the bottle for relief. As it is often the case, alcohol did not offer any comfort. It made matters worse. The more he drank, the worse his ability to sustain healthy intimacy with his partners became. As he spoke about his needs, desires, pain, and frustration, I could not help but wonder what had brought Mark to such state of desperation. By this time, at the fairly young age of thirty-two, he had lost all hope to ever having a family. He had concluded that one day he would be found dead in a drunken stupor. And yet, there we were trying to find an exit door.

I wanted to know, obviously, what event or events had sent him off into this journey of despair. As it happens in many cases, this could have been a case of systematic physical abuse by his mother or some other form of sexual abuse by a relative or family friend. I wanted to know why he could not maintain healthy intimate relationships with women, and with people in general. There was no question Mark's intimacy mechanism was severely damaged and it was in desperate need of restoration.

Mark's story began when he caught his mother cheating on his father with another man when he was seven. His father was a truck driver who spent long hours and days away from home. He remembered his father as a hard worker and a kind man. His father always had time for him when he was around, and he still maintained a very close relationship with him. One night, Mark was woken by some loud noises coming from his parents' bedroom. He knew his father was not home, so, he decided to investigate. He approached the bedroom door and tried to push it open, but there was an object blocking the door. However, he pushed harder and was able to take a look at the scene of his mother engaged in sexual relationships with a stranger. Mark became very afraid and very angry. He went back to his room without knowing what to do. He could not tell his father that there was this man in his bed with his mother. He felt helpless and impotent. Mark began to notice that several different men would frequently come to spend time with his mother. Over the years, he was aware that his mother had been involved with multiple men. He could hear the men coming into the house and, sometimes, staying the night while his father was away with his truck. Mark had never told the story to anyone until that day in my office. Even though his parents divorced when he was about fourteen, he never told his father what he had seen. He simply believed his father figured it out on his own and had chosen to divorce his mother as a result. Mark told me that since the day he saw his mother with another man, he had believed that all women are *whores.*

Obviously, the irreconcilable contradiction created by his mother's infidelity pushed Mark to believe the lie that women were not trustworthy. He was living with a second contradiction in that he had the desperate need for emotional and spiritual intimacy with women he considered to be unworthy. Mark was trapped, and he turned to the bottle to self-medicate his terrible pain. His contradiction was the result of a catastrophic spiritual injury even though he did not suffer any physical pain or sexual abuse. He probably survived for most of those years because he had a good father that gave the guidance he needed. And yet, he was not able to get rid of the memories that haunted him to this day. It is very probable that keeping his mother's secret did more damage to his intimacy mechanism than anything his mother had done. Mark needed to heal, and he needed to heal very fast.

Spiritual Injuries Roadmap

We have defined two types of spiritual injuries: the superficial (non-character altering) and the catastrophic (character altering). Both types leave permanent marks in people's soul, but only catastrophic injuries produce irreconcilable contradictions that turn into discernible blind spots. These blind spots find expression through a subconscious lie that guide people's behaviors that prevents them from seeing the correlation between the traumatic event and the corresponding dysfunctions. Catastrophic events have three very visible results. The trauma produces the initial effect of a state of confusion I have defined as the foggy field. After the foggy field experience has begun to subside, a blind spot begins to form that is expressed in a lie that prevents injured people from protecting themselves from instinctive reactions and persistent temptations. And finally, the trauma alters the person's character causing atrophy to the intimacy mechanism. The severity of the damage to the intimacy mechanism will determine people's ability to be involved in healthy and trusting relationships with others. The net result is that without transparency, people cannot develop healthy intimate relationships. This was, clearly, Mark's case. He went through all these three stages, and the end result was that his intimacy mechanism was severely damaged by the contradiction his mother's infidelity created in him.

The intimacy mechanism is essential for healthy sociological functioning. God designed human beings to be fully engaged in healthy intimate relationships with God and others. This is one of the reasons the Bible puts such a strong emphasis on reconciliation. God sent Jesus to reconcile us back unto himself (Jn. 3:16; Rom. 5:8). In turn, Jesus taught that we have to forgive each other's offenses in response to his forgiveness of ours. Jesus taught us to pray this way: "Forgive our debts as we also forgive our debtors" (Matt. 6:12). Most people interpret Jesus's words about forgiveness from an exclusively *spiritual* perspective. But I believe forgiveness is as crucial for our peace of mind as it is to our intimacy with God. In other words, forgiving "our debtors" restores us to a deeper walk with God, but also to a healthier perception of God's image in us. God expects us to extend forgiveness to others to the same extent we have experienced God's forgiveness, for this is the only way we can find peace and joy. Alan Brandt was quoted as saying that "being resentful, they say, is like taking poison and waiting for the other person to die."[26] Pam W. Vredevelt and Kathryn Rodriguez said that "stuffing anger

---

[26]   Alan Brandt, 1995.

away is like holding hot coal in your hands. You will get burned."[27] Their message is that resentment, which is holding on to anger for unresolved conflicts, will hurt us more than it would hurt the person who is the object of our resentment. If we want to cleanse ourselves from the dangers of anger and resentment, there is one remedy—forgiveness.

I will expand on the forgiveness concept in Chapter 7. But suffice here to say that the intimacy mechanism cannot be fully restored without experiencing and extending forgiveness. Without forgiveness, the resentment and anger will remain. And these two feelings are poisoning our hearts. They prevent us from moving forward into living a full of life. Forgiveness is not just a nice Christian principle. It is the essential element that restores a broken heart to love again. If we are going to enter into intimate relationships with God and others, we must learn how to leave our past where it belongs, in the past. Forgiveness has two crucial elements: (1) breaking the stranglehold the past has on the present, and (2) preventing past mistakes or injuries to determine who we will become.

When the intimacy mechanism is damaged, we feel like a fish out of water—separated from his natural habitat. Our social context is defined through our relationships. And when people are separated from their spiritual and social context, they lose their life source which is their spiritual connection with God and others. Since isolation and loneliness are the antithesis of intimacy, people cannot function properly when they are alone. As we have mentioned earlier, God intentionally created mankind for intimacy because, "it is not good for man to be alone" (Gen. 2:18). The sooner we understand that God's image in us means that we were created to love and be loved, the sooner we can enter into the healing process that will restore our fellowship with God and others.

Most of us remember the story of Cain and Abel. Cain killed his brother out of jealousy. Cain had seen that God was pleased with Abel's sacrifice while rejecting his. The inspired writer tells us that when God asked Cain for Abel's whereabouts, Cain tried to deflect responsibility for his actions. When God pressed the issue

---

27   Pam W. Vredevelt and Kathryn Rodriguez. *Surviving the Secret*, 1987.

against him, Cain responded by asking, "Am I my brother's keeper?" (Gen. 4:9). With his own question, Cain pronounced judgment on himself. The question did not need an answer because Cain's guilt was established by his own words. Abel's murder is a profound event that established the rudimentary need to respect our neighbor's life and dignity. I believe that out of Cain's question emerges the commandment: "Thou shall not murder" (Ex. 20:13). Jesus later expanded the commandment further. He said, "You have heard that it was said thou shall not murder, but I tell you that anyone who hates his brother is subject to judgment" (Matt. 5:21-22). Jesus clarified the law. The commandment was not given to curve conduct. It was given to transform the conscience, but Israel's leaders had stopped short of God's purpose. The people misunderstood the spirit of the law because they stayed, on the superficial aspect of the law. They focused on the letter of the law that results in death, instead of the spirit of the law that brings life.

Being our brother's keeper was an admonition *against* harming others. Jesus's teaching in the parable of the Good Samaritan affirms the principle to "love your neighbor as yourself" (Lk. 10:27-28). I believe Jesus's intent was to take the principle a step further. Jesus's point was to encourage us to intentionally seek our neighbor's good. It is not sufficient to avoid harming others. Loving others is an intentional and proactive choice to show mercy and grace to others. It is in this context that God expects us to express forgiveness and agape love. Jesus added that people would know that we are his disciples in that "we love one another" (Jn. 13:34-35). I believe that love is the most fundamental of all of God's relational character qualities. As such, love demands forgiveness as the bridge to reconnect us with God and people.

Dysfunctional Intimacy

Let's address the damaged intimacy mechanism and see how we can find possible solutions that minimize the impairment that keep many people from developing healthy expressions of intimacy with God and others. Some people think Jesus's words to love "your neighbor as you love yourself" are too difficult to actually live by. He left us a tough standard, without a doubt. Yet he knew that unless we can overcome the tendency to dwell in our resentment, we would have difficulties finding fulfillment for our lives. I believe that healthy intimacy is not possible without trust, which in turn depends on honesty, which it depends on being transparent with others. Therefore, engaging others with agape love requires that people get rid of the resentment that resides in their souls. The solution is the art of forgiveness.

I have seen plenty of people on their last days and hours. I never heard anyone express the desire that they should have spent more time at work digging ditches. Most of the people I have seen pass away have expressed to me the desire to spend more time with family and friends or doing more good deeds for people. We can see this at a larger scale when rich people dedicate most of their last days on earth giving their wealth to charities. These people share their wealth for two main reasons: First, they have concluded that they cannot take their wealth with them. Second, they have also realized that helping their fellow man gives them significance and brings them joy.

As the readers may have already noticed, loving our neighbors is not done solely for the neighbor's benefit. On the contrary, loving others is the foundation for healthy reciprocal relationships that mirror God's eternal relationship within the Trinity. That is, people look more like Jesus when they are engaged in loving relationships with God and others. Our lives lose a touch of their meaning without agape love, which is maximum expression of God's character in his relationship to man. As long as God's love is not flowing through us, the relational impairment remains. Paul's prayer for the Philippian church stated: "And this is my prayer: that your love may abound more and more in knowledge and depth of insight so that you may be able to discern what is best" (Phil. 1:9-10a). Paul made a direct connection between growing in love and having "knowledge and depth of insight." In other words, our spiritual growth is directly linked to our ability to love God and to love others. As we grow in love, we grow into the kind of person God designed us to be.

We can only experience and share God's agape love within the context of healthy and transparent relationships. The following statement is key: Relational spiritual injuries have the effect of cursing people back to the time when they were out of fellowship with God. It is not a stretch to interpret God's words to mean that in spite of his freedom and relationship with God, Adam had experienced loneliness before God created Eve. And God used Adam's loneliness as a guide to create Eve. This means that Adam should have known better than to leave Eve to act on her own in her relationship with the serpent. In other words, since Adam was present when Eve took the forbidden fruit, this action should have been a decision made by both. Adam abdicated his responsibilities by letting Eve take a lead role. And Eve usurped her responsibility by making a unilateral decision to eat of the forbidden fruit.

I imagine God allowed this short period of loneliness to teach Adam the lesson that he had a natural longing for companionship. Adam's lonely days were not the good old days. Obviously not all spiritual injuries have this ultimate result, but loneliness is the default mode of a broken intimacy mechanism. People's inability to heal from their spiritual injuries leads them toward isolation. I suggest to you that when people suffer crippling spiritual injuries, that result in permanent damage to the intimacy mechanism, they become dysfunctional in their natural environment of transparent relationships.

Restoration Through Worship

King David had assembled a team of singers and poets to lead worship as members of the tabernacle's choir (1 Chr. 6:31-32). A man named Asaph was among the worship leaders David had put together, and he appeared to have taken a leading role in worship. According to 2 Chr. 29:30, both, David and Asaph were accomplished singers and poets. The Bible has preserved many of David's psalms, and at least one of Asaph's psalms. Asaph established a school for poets and singers and those who followed him as worship leaders were called "the sons of Asaph" (1 Chr. 25:1; Ezra 2:41). Today's church musicians and worship leaders can be considered "spiritual children of Asaph."

Asaph wrote one of the most insightful psalms in the Bible. Psalm 73 details Asaph's inner struggles with his doubts about God's goodness toward him. He knew, and believed, that God was good to Israel. He also knew that God's plan for his people would be fulfilled, and he looked to the future of the nation with hope. But Asaph's struggle was more personal. He could not see God's hand working in his daily life. Listen how he described his journey on the valley of faith.

> Truly God is good to Israel, to those who are pure in heart. But as for me, my feet had almost stumbled, my steps had nearly slipped. For I was envious of the arrogant when I saw the prosperity of the wicked (Ps. 73:1-3).

Asaph had become depressed. He could have judged God's lack of action against those whom he believed were wicked men, and he began to question God's goodness toward him. The wicked were prospering, according to Asaph, while he who had dedicated his entire life to worship in the tabernacle, languished without hearing from God. The psalmist goes on to say how his doubts were proven truthful by the actions of the wicked. He had lost his self-esteem. He could not see God's grace in his music and worship.

Asaph's problem was that he, like many of us today, was judging his relationship with God through the lenses of his own suffering while comparing himself to other people. He had forgotten, for a season, that his worth as a person did not come from others' opinions or successes. Rather, his worth came from the Lord. But he had to struggle with his own self-worth in relationship to God in order to find his true value from God. After his season of struggle, Asaph tells us that he returned to the sanctuary. His outlook on life changed. In the temple, he saw the real meaning of his worship and value. Read it with me. "But when I thought how to understand this, it seemed to me a wearisome task, until I went into the sanctuary of God; then I discerned their end" (Ps. 73:16-17).

In the sanctuary of God, the psalmist rediscovered his value and worth through worship. He then, concluded with the following words: "Whom have I in heaven but you? And there is nothing on earth that I desire besides you" (Ps. 73:25). In his rediscovery of worship as the means to reestablish his relationship with God, Asaph's spirit was lifted to its proper perspective. If, like the psalmist, we are going to be restored to full spiritual health, in which we can have sincere intimacy with God and others, we have to recognize the three spiritual truths at work here.

First, we have to recognize God's goodness toward us. During his struggle, Asaph could accept God's goodness to others, but he could not see it as applying to himself. But God's goodness is not distributed arbitrarily. God is good, and he is good to me, as an individual, who was created in his image. The second truth is that we cannot discern God's goodness through comparing ourselves with other people. Asaph almost lost his footing (he said: "my feet almost slipped") because he lost sight of God's actions in his life. He was spending too much time watching how the wicked prospered, and he had missed God's movement in his own life. Finally, we must accept God's goodness as being intrinsic to who he is. This means that God *cannot not be good.* Thus, when Asaph entered the temple and he recognized God's goodness toward him, he was able to see "the end of the wicked." In other words, he did not have to be concerned with God's ability to judge justly. All he needed to do was live his life in God's presence and let God take care of the rest.

Worship provides the solution to the problems of unworthiness and low self-esteem. Worship is an event based on a transparent relationship with God. It gives us access to the creator. It also reveals how valuable we are to God, thus, affirming that our self-esteem comes from God. Once we know we are valuable, regardless of the events that may have damaged us, we can overcome the fears and anxieties of feeling unworthy. It is imperative that we do not let those who have used their power to hurt us, to define us. God has already defined us as persons who are able to enter into intimate relationships with him. The fact that our intimacy mechanism has been broken by spiritual injuries is a definite obstacle to our restoration. But this is the reason we must return to the temple where we can find our true identity in God.

The critical point here is that God designed us to be in fellowship with him and with others. In this designed God gave us the ability to love and be loved. Therefore, God is the one that defines our worth to him. He gave us worth when he shared his personhood qualities with us. Since God gave us value, then, no person has the power to take that away from us. It is imperative that we always evaluate who we are in light of God's design and not in light of other people's opinions. This is the essence of our restoration. Our self-worth comes from God's image in us, and not from the violence done to us by a perpetrator or by our circumstances.

The Church as a Healing Place

The apostle John made very strong accusations against one of the churches in Asia. He said to Laodicea: "I know your deeds, that you are neither cold nor hot. I wish you were either one or the other! So, because you are lukewarm—neither hot nor cold—I am about to spit you out of my mouth" (Rev. 3:15-16). According to John, Laodicea's testimony had become nauseating. When God would look at this church, he would feel like throwing up. Let me give you some background.

The city of Laodicea was located in Asia Minor. This city had become the center for ophthalmology, the textile and banking industries. Laodicea was a favorite stop for merchants and for people seeking relief for all types of vision problems. The city, however, had one big problem. Since it only had a few streams of flowing water that would dry up during the hot summer months, the city was virtually without drinking water during those months.

However, Laodicea had two sister cities, Colossae to the northeast, and Hierapolis to the northwest. Both of these cities had plenty of running water. They also had other advantages. For instance, Colossae had very cold springs of water all year round. Armies would stop by Colossae to drink their exquisite cold waters. Hierapolis, on the other hand, had wells of extremely hot waters that were used by passersby for medicinal purposes. Colossae's waters refreshed. Hierapolis's waters healed.

In order to have water flowing during the summer months, Laodicea had commissioned building two aqueducts, one from Colossae and one from Hierapolis, to bring water to the city. However, as a result of the distance, by the time the waters from Colossae arrived at Laodicea, they would be lukewarm. The same phenomenon would happen with the waters from Hierapolis. Their hot waters would also cool off while traveling to Laodicea also arriving lukewarm. Even though Laodicea craved the much-needed waters, the distance made them almost undrinkable.

The apostle John, in a masterful piece of literature, was comparing the gospel message of the church of Laodicea, not to the waters in Colossae or Hierapolis, but to the lukewarm waters they had to drink from the city's reserves. The church's message had become undrinkable. It neither had the refreshing power of the waters from Colossae ("you are not cold"), nor the healing power of the waters of Hierapolis ("you are not hot"). Jesus revealed to John that he wished the church's message could refresh (to be cold) or to heal (to be hot). But Laodicea had become complacent and had accepted the wishy-washy message that compromised the gospel, and as a result it had lost all power to have meaningful impact on the city to which they had been called to serve. The church, therefore, is a place in which people can find cold waters to quench their thirst, or hot waters in which they can find healing.

Not only had the church lost her healing and refreshing power, they had become boastful and proud. The Laodiceans had confused their external blessings, associated with the city, with their spiritual blessings. John called them on this attitude. Listen how John described the church's worldliness. "You say, 'I am rich; I have acquired wealth and do not need a thing.' But you do not realize that you are wretched, pitiful, poor, blind and naked" (Rev. 3:17). The church claimed to be rich because the city of Laodicea was rich. The banking industry brought a great deal of wealth to the city, but the church was spiritually poor. The church claimed to see, because the city of Laodicea was known for her ophthalmological advances, but the church was spiritually blind. The church claimed to be clothed because of Laodicea's excellent textile industry, but they were spiritually naked. The church could not heal, and they could not refresh.

Then, John proceeded to tell them what they needed to do. He said: "I counsel you to buy from me gold refined in the fire, so you can become rich; and white clothes to wear, so you can cover your shameful nakedness; and salve to put on your eyes, so you can see" (Rev. 3:18). John was calling the church to repentance. He wanted them to return to the message of the gospel and to stop measuring their success based on their city's wealth. The church needed to repent and become the refreshing and healing place they once were.

This is another reason that restoration to spiritual health comes through worship, or through a return to God. We find our true identity and purpose in our relationship with God. This is the reason we cannot allow other people to define our worth because it does not come from them. Our worth comes from the Lord. This was true about Asaph and Laodicea, and it is true about us today. When we become distracted by other people's successes, we have the tendency to measure our worth through them. But when we focus our attention on the gospel message, and keep our eyes on Jesus, we will be rich, clothed, and we will see clearly God's actions on our behalf.

Spiritual Traumas Are Unique

While science has treated mental health issues for centuries, spiritual injuries do not necessarily become a mental illness, although many of them become crippling dysfunctions. As such, they cannot always be effectively treated as a mental health issue. Spiritual brokenness requires a spiritual approach to healing. In this book, I am not speaking about the use of the divine healing gift per se, even though I do not rule that out. My focus is to draw from the healing power inherent within the community of faith. Paul described the church as a "body" (Eph. 3:6). Paul's use of this metaphor is significant because God created the physical body with self-healing properties. The body heals broken bones. It has the ability to stop bleeding and close flesh wounds. It fights infections, viruses, and all kinds of bacteria.

If the physical body is overwhelmed with trauma, the damage could be permanent and even fatal. Spiritually speaking, the same phenomenon takes place. When people suffer smaller spiritual injuries, their recovery is shorter and do not leave permanent damage to the intimacy mechanism.

The church (the Body of Christ) needs to be the spiritual place in which people can experience the restoration of the broken intimacy mechanism and reestablish a balanced perception of self. Jesus declared that "in this, the world will know you are my disciples, if you love one another" (Jn. 13:35). No other human activity has greater healing power than love. When the church does not exhibit Jesus's love in her daily interaction with the world and with its members, the church has lost her healing or refreshing power. The church is not just an example of Jesus's love. The church is the place in which we are restored to spiritual health through fellowship (loving neighbor) and through worship (loving God).

The church needs to encourage healthy and intimate relationships that make trusting each other safe again. Our worship needs to be Christ-centered in order to create an environment for sincere fellowship. When our worship is focused on God, we are restored to a higher expression of love—agape love. In our worship, we meet Jesus as our Savior, and we can see our neighbor as a child of God bearing his image. God cannot help himself. He simply has to love us. Love is one of God's character-defining qualities. That's who he is. His healing power will flow through the Body of Christ, as we love one another. As long as worship is centered in our relationship with God, and away from us, we can regain the proper alignment with him and begin to trust again. That's the purpose of worship, to restore our proper alignment with God. This alignment means that we have a clear understanding that God is God and that we are not God.

This understanding must include the recognition that God is worthy of worship. Worship is the spiritual event in which people are restored to an intimate relationship with God. Worship is the highest spiritual form of intimacy with God because it is the accurate acknowledgment of God's role as creator and our roles as the created. Worship clarifies who we are in our reciprocal relationship with God. As such, when Jesus spoke about loving God, he was making reference to the essential element of transparency. Sincere reciprocal intimacy is not possible until trust is established as the bridge of reconciliation between two parties that are in conflict. If we want to bring our lives to balance, we need to practice agape love. Agape is, both, worship "in spirit and in truth," and it is fellowship when we "love our neighbor as ourselves." The balance is struck, in my estimation, when worship and fellowship are founded upon reconciliation with our neighbor and spiritual and emotional transparency with God.

The church can also assist in restoring people's self-image through the preaching of the gospel message that is based on the revelation that we were "created in God's image" (Gen. 1:27). If people were similar to animals, lacking any spiritual or emotional connection with God, our restoration to a healthy self-image would become virtually impossible. How can people, with the personhood qualities of self-awareness, conscience, and purpose, raise their self-esteem if their ancestors are his inherently inferiors because they lack those personhood qualities? People's self-esteem can only be raised when we live for a purpose higher than ourselves.

Our creation in God's image elevates us to a higher category of life. People can only be restored to a renewed understanding of who he is in light of God's creation. This is the reason that our worship, as an expression of gratefulness for God's grace, his forgiveness, and our restoration to fellowship with God through Christ, is fundamental for a higher expression of self. Each one of us must be encouraged and taught to adjust our thinking in light of God's character and not in light of our brokenness. This is the reason the Apostle John said, "If anyone says, 'I love God,' and hates his brother, he is a liar; for he who does not love his brother whom he has seen cannot love God whom he has not seen" (1 Jn. 4:20). We desire a higher expression of self. God offers us the higher expression through a transparent relationship with him. Evolution, on the other hand, offers us a lower expression of self by using primates as our aspiration. If you don't mind, I will stay with God.

CHAPTER 7
Spiritual Health: Becoming Whole

We have journeyed through the definition of spiritual injuries, their causes, and their consequences. For some readers, this may have been a fun exercise because they were able to discover minor pet peeves that have caused minor anxieties over the years. For other readers, this book might have been a painful experience because it forced them to recall long gone events that are still haunting them to this day. If you find yourself thinking about ways to overcome your defensiveness, your instinctive reactions, and how to overcome persistent temptations, then, we have achieved one of our main objectives, which is to recognize the presence of blind spots caused by catastrophic spiritual injuries. Clearly, the healing process cannot begin until the initial external symptoms have been identified. If spiritual injuries have impacted your life in a deeper way than you ever thought, then you are ready to take the next steps in the healing process, which has as its ultimate goal to restore your intimacy mechanism, so you can be whole again. In our context, wholeness is understood as people's ability to love with agape love that allows them to establish healthy spiritual and emotional intimacy with God and others.

The healing process described in this book is intentionally biblical in that it draws its principles from the human experience as revealed in Scripture. The Bible is the best source of information to describe God's character as well as the human condition. The biblical stories, prophecies, poems, and struggles, form the nucleus that reveal who we are in our broken state. But those same narratives tell the story of our need to be in communion with God. The psalmist captured this sentiment when he said: "As a deer pants for flowing streams, so pants my soul for you, O God" (Ps. 42:1). This unquenchable thirst described David's deep desire for God. Only being in God's presence could have quenched David's spiritual thirst. He either had God, or his soul would dry up without him.

I believe the biblical stories are more than simplistic narrations of human events, or fantastic events in which God was the primary mover. I also believe the Holy Spirit specifically inspired the stories we find in the Bible as indicators of human behavioral patterns. The stories are also indicators (signs) that give people directions on how to return to God. These stories give context to our spiritual journey, which is always concerned with getting us back into fellowship with God.

These biblical stories are educational instruments that reveal God's insights into the human character. The stories present a correct or a distorted view of our human nature depending on people's spiritual or emotional proximity to God. The greater our spiritual distance from God, the greater the danger of ending up like the prodigal son, eating pods with pigs. The closer our proximity with God, the greater the joy of feasting at the Father's table. Biblical stories also present a grim but sober exposition of the human condition in the current state of rebellion against God and on our neglect for our fellow man. And yet, from within our rebellion against God, biblical stories also reveal our desperate need to have peace with him. The biblical picture is not intended to leave us in despair. On the contrary, God knows that unless we come to grips with our present condition of willful disobedience, we cannot take the necessary steps of repentance and confession to be reconciled with him.

In addition to describing the human condition, these biblical stories establish the path that can lead people to spiritual health and to experience a full restoration to intimacy with God. This is the reason, that in addition to the biblical stories, I have used people's stories to illustrate the different levels of brokenness spiritual traumas have produced. Let me share with you two foundational truths that determine our ability to relate to God.

First, the Bible declares that, "all have sinned and have fallen short of the glory of God" (Rom. 3:23). Paul's statement to the Romans is a summary of Adam's story at the Garden of Eden. Like Adam and

Eve each one of us has chosen to "eat of the tree of the knowledge of good and evil." The immediate consequence of Adam's sin was his shame, which removed him from God's presence. Like it happens with all spiritual injuries, Adam and Eve established several lies to excuse their desire to *hide* from God. Of course, no one really hides from God, even if they are delusional enough to believe they can. Read with me how Paul described our separation from God. We were once "alienated and hostile in mind, doing evil deeds" (Col. 1:21). Did you catch Paul's words? We were "hostile [to God] in our minds." We had believed the lie that God did not have our best interests in mind. Our hostility against God created a barrier, in our minds, that blocked our communion with God and became an impenetrable wall until Jesus tore it down at the cross.

Second, God has provided a remedy that overcomes the sinful human condition and brings people into a reconciled relationship with God. Salvation is more than just a psychological or sociological human need. It is the gift of God to all who believe in Jesus's redeeming work. God made salvation available to every person on the basis of faith in Christ. God has reconciled the world unto himself through Christ. Since Jesus's death cleansed the world from the stain of sin, the sin barrier is no longer the insurmountable obstacle that can keep us alienated from God.

God created us to exist in relationships, both with him and with others. Thus, our full restoration with God must also include fellowship with the people around us. Our journey on this earth is marked with a struggle with sin and temptations. However, we can be restored to a proper relationship with God and live successfully in hope through the process of repentance and reconciliation.

The Healing Process

I do not exaggerate when I say that most of us have experienced some form of spiritual trauma. However, not everyone has experienced the same level of brokenness. The intensity of people's emotional responses to their original injuries is a determinative factor on how extensive the damage to the intimacy mechanism has become. People can also discern how severely damaged they are, by the intensity of their emotional reactivity and defensiveness to certain events and people.

For example, I met a couple on their road to divorce. They had three children, a twelve-years old girl, a six-years old boy, and a four years old boy. I met with the couple on several occasions, but they were convinced that they could not reconcile, not even for the children's sake. They were concerned with their twelve-years old girl. She had become withdrawn and was having problems at school. I met with the oldest daughter, and in a very short time I realized, that she was having mixed feelings about the divorce. On the one hand, she did not want the parents to divorce because she loved them both. She stated that they had been good to the children, but not good to each other. On the other hand, she had grown tired of all the fighting and wanted it to stop. She told me that all she wanted was for the whole charade to be over. I did not talk with the younger boys, but they appeared to be oblivious to the impending divorce or what that would mean to them.

In this case, the younger boys, who had not suffered through all the fighting, could be more damaged by the divorce than their oldest sibling because they would experience the divorce as a reflection on them. The contradiction would be more intense for them, precisely, because they will not be able to reconcile their beliefs and their reality. However, the oldest daughter, who had suffered through twelve years of fights, would be damaged differently than her brothers. She will feel some relief regarding the divorce. She has grown tired of the fights and she is ready to end the ordeal, even if she suffers some damage later. Her younger siblings were on the initial stages of recognizing the severity of the issues plaguing their family, but the older sister was already past that stage. By the time the divorce became effective, the oldest sister had already experienced several spiritual injuries along the way. The younger children could not understand why their parents needed to go their separate ways and leave them feeling abandoned. This feeling of abandonment often results in additional collateral spiritual injuries for all the siblings.

An infinite number of variables contributes to the confusion and difficulty in describing the intensity of the trauma and its resulting consequences. This is the reason we need to treat each person's spiritual trauma as being unique. No two-people's brokenness is identical, even when they have a shared experience. Additionally, the injuries are unique because no one can duplicate the personal life experiences, or the emotional reactions, of another. The uniqueness of the trauma makes the restoration journey extremely difficult because people don't have a cookie cutter method that can be applied equally to every person. But, the process of identifying the symptoms produced by the trauma is also fairly simple because collective human behavior can become very predictable. This works toward the church's advantage. The church can pinpoint the issues fairly quickly to intervene in the healing process to give hope to the brokenhearted.

I think we are now ready to discuss the five elements of the healing process. It's time to take the necessary steps to repair the intimacy mechanism. I present each element in a logical progression, but we can work on more than one at a time, and on occasions we could move up and down the line to complete a previous element as new information emerges. Join me.

First Element: Personal Inventory

The first element in the healing process is to prepare a personal inventory. This inventory focuses on the life events that may have left permanent and recognizable emotional scars. At this stage of the process, we are not concerned with the severity of any particular trauma or event. The most important aspect of this step is to identify the events themselves. Once people have listed all the events they can remember, they can begin to identify the feelings associated with those events and how those events may have marked them for life. During this process, people would be able to discern how these events may have caused them to become defensive or overly reactive to certain events and situations.

When people begin to write their most significant experiences, in all likelihood, they will describe the events that left the biggest impressions. People have the tendency to prioritize events based on their emotional significance, or to put them in chronological order.

As a practical matter, it does not matter how people put their stories together because they will always remember the most significant events, both, the ones with the most negative consequences, as well as the ones that left a very positive influence in them. As people write their significant events, either, they would be able to identify the emotionally negative scars or those that left emotionally positive impressions. If people describe the events, mostly, from their negative consequences, we can conclude that a specific event left an identifiable spiritual scar. As discussed earlier, spiritual scars are the resulting negative emotional responses to events. The individual's emotional response to the event is the most direct correlation between the trauma and the resulting scar (or memory). In other words, the higher is the person's emotional identification with an event, the deeper the injury.

Earlier I shared my accident at the end of the Jungle Expert Training in Panama. I have connected my fear of heights to that event. Since I do not remember any other event that could have impacted my fears of heights, I feel that accident was instrumental to condition my thinking. Is it possible that a different event could have contributed to my fear of heights? Of course! Anything is possible. But the only event that I can remember with excruciating detail, that could have left, both, a physical scar and a negative emotional response to heights, is the fall in Panama. While my fear of heights developed gradually, it took me years to confess to myself that I was in fact, afraid of heights, even after I recognized my reactions. I could see how I avoided events or situations that could put me on the edge of a building or on a tall ladder. The benefit of telling this story is that once I accepted my fear of heights, it did not take long before I made the connection with the accident in Panama.

The personal inventory should focus on easily remembered events. Once we have made our list, we can add more obscure events that could also have left emotional reactions. If we are not sure of what events we can add to the list, we could also list situations that we know make us susceptible to persistent temptations or events we remember in which we reacted with strong defensiveness. Once we have made a list of the events, we want to work our way back to identify other possible injuries that we may have *forgotten*. Please remember that we never forget anything. We simply file certain things away and never open that file drawer again. If one of these forgotten events was catastrophic, then, this is an event we must eventually deal with, because it may have the key to the lie the blind spot created. This could be a tedious process, but if it is done carefully, it can produce tremendous results. So, don't get discouraged or overly concerned at what you might discover. After people have identified several major events, they will be in a better position to move to the second element in the healing process.

Second Element: Acceptance

Once the personal inventory has brought to light the possible spiritual injuries with their accompanying scars and blind spots, we can begin to identify the level of damage the trauma has caused to the intimacy mechanism. This is the aspect of the human experience that is most directly affected by relational traumas. When the intimacy mechanism is out of balance, people can have difficulties relating to God and others.

Acceptance is a crucial step in the healing process, mostly, because people cannot move through the healing process without recognizing that the trauma left serious damage along its path. Acceptance is not a remedy for people's inability to recognize their brokenness. Generally speaking, injured people do not deny they had experienced a spiritual injury, even if they don't have the terminology that can help them define the trauma. There might be a confusion in relationship to the circumstances or the motives that made the injury possible, but most people readily recognize the injury itself.

For example, a woman could be in denial as it relates to the consequences of a rape. She could claim that the she is over the pain associated with the rape, or she can even deny that the rape changed her in any significant way. She could even claim the rape was her fault. But she cannot be in denial regarding the event itself. That memory (scar) is clearly seared into her consciousness. I recognize that some events could be so horrific that some people can bury them so deeply in their subconscious that remembrance of the event is a hit and miss proposition. These cases are rare, but we cannot ignore that they exist. That said, I operate from the perspective that most people remember the critical events that may have produced the irreconcilable contradiction that resulted in a spiritual injury. This is the reason we start the healing process by identifying the lie hidden behind the blind spots and work our way back to the contradiction created by the trauma that produced the spiritual injury.

Acceptance in this context is a reference to coming to terms with the damage people have experienced to their intimacy mechanism. A secondary aspect of the acceptance stage is recognizing how the trauma might have eroded the perception of self-worth. When people feel rejected by others, they tend to evaluate their motives through the distorted intimacy mechanism caused by the trauma. The brokenhearted experience leaves people with three specific issues: unworthiness, mistrust, and a sense of indignity. These three elements must be repaired before people can engage in healthy intimate relationships with God and people. As long as any one of these three elements is missing or remains damaged, people cannot find emotional fulfillment.

I believe self-preservation (or self-love) is a fundamental truth about the human experience. This would mean that anyone with a damaged intimacy mechanism, who experiences the accompanying feelings of unworthiness, would have difficulties loving others. It is impossible to give something we don't have, and loving others without having a healthy attitude about our inherent dignity and self-worth, is virtually impossible. Additionally, people could develop the tendency to filter every life event through their distorted view of self. If people realize their difficulties establishing healthy intimacy, then, it is imperative to acknowledge that both the intimacy mechanism and the self-worth have suffered severe damage. The damage prevents them from experiencing healthy intimate relationships with neighbors and God. Since God created us to live in loving relationships, we cannot find fulfillment as long as we understand our dignity and self-worth from the perspective of being broken.

When God said, "It is not good for man to be alone," he was not declaring that he had just come up with a new brilliant idea. God's creation of man was male and female. This is a significant point. From

God's perspective the word man is not a reference to the male side of the equation. *Man* is both, male and female. At the beginning, God put Adam through a process of lack of companionship to show him his need for social interaction. Adam might have told God something like, "Look here, God, all the animals have partners, except me. Is there something we can do about this?" God said, "You are right. Let me create a companion for you." After Adam had accepted his need for companionship, God created Eve, and with her appearance, God defined and established the parameter for human interaction and relationships. Therefore, it is not good for man (the male or the female) to be alone. As stated earlier, the most significant result of spiritual injuries is the damage done to the intimacy mechanism, which in turn, results in spiritual and emotional isolation. This takes place when people feel alone in their crowded social environment. The issue is not lack of opportunities to engage others in healthy emotional intimacy. The issue is that people become unable to engage those who might be willing to join them on their journey. Thus, individuals must accept the reality of the damage caused by their spiritual trauma in order to move to the next healing element.

The Third Element: Confession

Confession is taking ownership and responsibility for our actions. This means that, even when our conduct was the result of the instinctive reactions caused by the spiritual injuries, we are still responsible for those actions. Taking responsibility for our actions is a critical element to recognize how much damage the trauma had caused. In other words, as long as we are avoiding taking responsibility for our actions, we can always blame the non-entity of an event we cannot identify. This confession is not intended to add guilt. Rather, the basic premise is that if we can accept responsibility for our actions, then, we can identify *the what and the how* of the spiritual injury. People need to know *what* type of damage the spiritual injury did to them. And they also need to know *how* it altered their characters. In many instances, if people can answer these two questions, they can have a better understanding how their journey moved from spiritual health into brokenness. Once people can see the path that took them to their brokenness, they will be able to see their way out to escape the rock bottom hell into which they have fallen.

Confession is a two-sided coin. When people make confession to God, they become free to reconcile with others. The other side of the equation is also true. When people make confession to others, for causing them harm, they become free to enter into God's presence without fear or false shame. Let me expand on this some more.

The goal of spiritual health is to escape the hopelessness created by the spiritual and emotional isolation produced by the trauma. The isolation is the external and visible result of a damaged intimacy mechanism. As we have established, God created us to be in healthy intimate relationships with him and with others. As such, the isolation Adam and Eve experienced at the Garden of Eden was not part of God's design for them. Adam and Eve chose isolation from God, even though they knew it was unhealthy for them. Their separation from God was so irreversible that biblical writers have described it as being dead. Nothing is more definite than death. Thus, separation from God brings spiritual death, and separation from others bring emotional death. As the intimacy mechanism begins to heal, finding hope becomes a real possibility for people. But we cannot escape the despair created by hopelessness until, or unless, we take ownership for our behaviors.

Therefore, we make confession to God for the wrongs we have done as the result of the spiritual injury so that we can reestablish the conditions that make intimacy with God possible. As we have stated earlier, transparency is the condition for sincere intimacy. As long as people have something to hide, they are not being transparent. Once people have accepted the pain associated with swallowing their pride and the embarrassment of accepting blame for their actions, they would have taken the first steps toward spiritual health. If you remember the parable of the prodigal son, the first thing he did was to "come to his senses." This is a masterful way of saying that he recognized he had hit rock bottom as a result of his own actions, and he needed to change direction. If you follow Luke's narrative, you can find that the next step for the prodigal was to "return to his father's house." And, during this process, the prodigal also did something spectacular. He said to himself that he would tell his father that he "had sinned against heaven and against him." This was a dual confession. He sinned against God and he had sinned against his father. Jesus's illustration ended with the father restoring the son to full fellowship. But if you noticed, the full fellowship could not have taken place without returning home and making the confession.

God provides and cares for us, but we in turn do violence against each other. Without God's goodness, we lose the meaning for our existence and assume that others have lost theirs, too. Therefore, we confess to become transparent before God. Confession also has the added benefit of removing the heavy burden of rebellion we have carried for years. Jesus said to "come to [him] those who are weary and heavy laden, and he would give [us] rest." The apostle John added that "if we confess our sins God is faithful and just to forgive us our sins…" (1 Jn. 1:9). For the purpose of our discussion, confession has two benefits. First, it allows us to take ownership of our actions. Second, it shines the light of revelation to the dysfunctional secrets we have carried for years.

The pertinent question the reader must be asking is; how can I confess for wrongs that are directly related to spiritual injuries? Is not my behavior instinctive and compulsive? How can it be my fault when I act under compulsion? These questions do not negate the need to confess. Rather, they affirm the need to confess. As long as people can blame others or their life circumstances for their actions, they will have a hard time being honest about who they have become. If they are always deflecting their responsibilities, they can never find out what the spiritual injury did to them and how it altered their characters. However, once people accept that their intimacy mechanism has been damaged by the spiritual trauma, then, they can accept that the injury has influenced their relationships and reactions to others. It is at this juncture that people can make the necessary choices to reverse the effects that the irreconcilable contradiction left in them. Please pay attention to the next statement. Until people have taken ownership for their behavior, regardless of the compulsion that brought it up, they cannot change said behavior.

If people deflect responsibility for their actions, or if they blame others for them, they will not have the emotional fortitude to overcome it. Let us say that your neighbor is stealing apples from his neighbor. That is not a behavior you have to make confession for or change. However, if you are the one stealing the apples from the neighbor, it does not matter the reasons that moved you to do it, you have to make confession for stealing the apples. The principle is that people can only make confession for what they have done. And they can only change behaviors for which they are responsible.

I believe that apologizing for other people's mistakes and behaviors is foolish. People must take ownership only for the things they are responsible. To whom do we make confessions? There are three possibilities to whom people should confess. First, we confess to ourselves. A confession to ourselves means that we take a look at ourselves in the mirror and accept that we have sinned against God and others. By this time, we have completed our personal inventory and have been able to identify how the spiritual injuries have conditioned our behavior. Therefore, what we are looking for here is to recognize that some of our compulsive behaviors were not acceptable, even if they were the result of instinctive and impulsive reactions directly connected to our blind spots. In other words, if I insult a waitress because she served a couple that clearly arrived after me, I can say that my reaction was instinctive. But insulting the waitress was still something I did, and I have to take ownership of it. Besides, it was the wrong thing to do.

When we make confession to ourselves, we bring into the open the undesirable behaviors that may have shamed us for years. This is not the time to point the blaming finger. This is the time to take ownership for our conduct. How do we know what type of behavior and attitude should people confess? If my attitude and conduct may have injured another person, I have to confess that to myself. If I want to clear my conscience, I need to acknowledge the wrong I have done, and seek forgiveness from the person I offended.

Second, we need to confess to God. How do we confess to God? The answer is not very complicated. Before we confess to God, we need to know within our souls what we are confessing. Sometimes people confess to God with platitudes like, "God you know all the wrongs I have done, forgive me." Well, that's nice, but that is not a confession. A confession is when we are able to list the specific activities and attitudes that have damaged us, have damaged our neighbor, and have violated God's love and character. Some people have come before the altar for confession and after one hour of tears not even God knows what they were trying to confess. There is a legitimate question that can be asked: What if the person does not know for sure what or how to confess? Then, they need to go back to the beginning. We can only make confession for that which we are conscious. If we are in doubt, let us figure it out first and then confess.

Third, we must confess the wrongs we have done to others. Jesus taught this principle during his teaching on the Sermon of the Mount. This confession is designed to mend the fences with others. Jesus stated:

> "If you are offering your gift at the altar and there remember that your brother has something against you, leave your gift there in front of the altar. First go and be reconciled to your brother; then come and offer your gift" (Matt. 5:23-24).

Most people interpret this passage to mean that we are the aggrieved party. After all, we are the ones bringing the offering to the altar. The interpretation that the innocent individuals should seek reconciliation with their brothers is asinine. It's important to note that the context argues against the interpretation that the innocent party initiates reconciliation. Jesus added:

> "Settle matters quickly with your adversary who is taking you to court. Do it while you are still with him on the way, or he may hand you over to the judge, and the judge may hand you over to the officer, and you may be thrown into prison." (Matt. 5:25)

As you can see, the context points in the opposite direction. I believe Jesus was encouraging us to reconcile with the adversary before *he* takes us to court. The only possible reason the adversary has a grievance against us has to be the result of an injury we inflicted on him. Therefore, if we are at the altar and there we recognize that a brother is taking us to court, because of something we have done to him, we should make every attempt to reconcile with the brother to avoid litigation in court. Jesus's point was not that the neighbor had injured us. Rather, it is that we had injured him, and he was taking us to court. We would be well advised to settle the neighbor's demands before bringing the offering to the altar. Jesus's point was that reconciling with our brother before going to court to collect on our offense is even more important than bringing the offering to the altar. Imagine that!

Before the prophet Nathan confronted David, the king did not feel the need to make confession and restitution. Did David know he had done wrong? Probably. Did he believe that his behavior, as king, merited confession? Probably not. God allowed the situation to go on for a while until he finally sent Nathan to confront David's sin. Once David understood God's position on the matter, he immediately turned to God in repentance.

Why is it important that people confess to God? The most important aspect of confessing to God is to express sadness for sins. God already knows when, where, and how often we have failed. It does not make any sense to try to hide our sins from him. God created this world as an agricultural system, and God knows perfectly well what the results are for any particular action or attitude. "A man reaps what he sows" (Gal. 6:7). If people have sown bad seeds by injuring other people, confession is a way to sow good seeds in God's kingdom to counter the negative harvest. In essence, we are asking God to work on our behalf to stop the negative harvest in favor of a positive one. It is important to remember that we confess to restore our standing in God's presence. That is, when we confess we are taking responsibility for our actions and our hearts are being cleansed of our wrongs.

There is an additional benefit to confessing to God. Confession lets God know that we have accepted accountability to him. With confession we acknowledge that he is the Lord of our lives. He knows this before we say it, but it is good for our souls to let him know. He expects certain responses from us. This reciprocal relationship provides the basis for the transformation of the mind to "conform us to the image of Christ" (Rom. 8:29). The desire, or pressure, to change becomes greater when we confess to God because we do not want to keep coming to him with shallow confessions about the same weakness over and over. However, if "we confess our sins, he is faithful and just and will forgive us our sins" (1 Jn. 1:9). God never gets tired of our confessions because he never gets tired of restoring us to fellowship.

The Fourth Element: Reconciliation

Reconciliation, in this context, has two main objectives. First, people need to find spiritual peace by achieving internal congruency between their glorified and real images of self. That is, injured individuals must bring the irreconcilable contradictions created by the spiritual injuries into harmony with their reality. It is crucial to realize that these conditions are not the norm for people's lives. Once people identify the injury for what it is, they will be ready to bring harmony to the spiritual turmoil caused by the contradiction.

Second, people need to receive God's forgiveness before they can offer reconciliation to others. Since God is the author of reconciliation of individuals with himself, they are not in a position to engage him in intense negotiations for the terms of reconciliation. Reconciliation is a gift. God declared that people are reconciled with him through faith. Faith, in its most simple definition, means to trust God's goodness. It is this trust in God's goodness that needs to be restored. Once people become convinced of God's goodness (and trust in him is restored), people can enter into his presence without the fear or the anxiety of rejection. Most people certainly have been rejected enough. When people confess, God is faithful to forgive all our unrighteousness. With reconciliation, we receive God's favor as demonstrated in Christ's sacrifice on the cross. When Paul implored people to be reconciled with God, he was making the appeal that we needed to reverse our rebellious course against God (2 Cor. 5:20).

At the moment people accept God's reconciliation, they are recognizing that God has their best interests in mind. He is committed to their good, and he is dedicated to restoring them to full fellowship with him. God's acceptance breaks the cycle of rejection and establishes people's true identity in God in spite of their brokenness. In other words, if God loved us while we were broken, how much more he will accept us now that he has begun the process of healing our broken hearts (Rom. 5:10).

The reader will notice that I did not include a section in which I encourage the injured person to pursue reconciliation with a perpetrator. There is one basic reason for the omission. In order for the victim to consider the possibility of reconciliation, the perpetrator must take the initiative by showing remorse for his actions through a repentance and confession process. In other words, it is not up to the victim to reach out to the perpetrator. The victim can choose to forgive the offense as an act of grace, but I strongly discourage the victim to initiate any reconciliation process with a perpetrator until they have overcome the effects of the spiritual injury. If the injured individuals reach out for reconciliation before their injuries have healed and their blind spots identified, they could experience a relapse. I am not suggesting the victims should hold a grudge or remain angry for the rest of their lives. On the contrary. I believe that once the victims have made confession and have been reconciled with God, they are in a better position to make other decisions. But since this process could take a lifetime, victims should not waste their time trying to reconcile with an unrepentant perpetrator.

One of the most misinterpreted passages of Scriptures is "love your enemies." Many people think that Jesus commandment to "love your enemies" means to become friends with them. Please read carefully. Jesus did not say, "Become friends with your enemies." He said to love them. The difference is immense. I do not believe it is humanly possible, or desirable, for a woman to become friends with her rapist. To have that expectation of her is not only foolish, it is cruel. Why would we expose her to more agony and suffering by being in the presence of her rapist?

Loving your enemy means that you will not seek his destruction through revenge, because revenge belongs to the Lord. If your enemy is found in a life and death situation, loving them could be as simple as dialing 911.

The Fifth Element: Forgiveness

Once we are in the process of achieving spiritual peace with ourselves and with God, we can then choose to extend forgiveness to our victimizer. Forgiveness is a *me* issue. We choose to forgive on our terms because the spiritual turmoil has subsided and there is no longer a need to seek revenge or to punish the perpetrator.

We must remember that forgiveness is always offered from a position of strength. That is, we do not forgive someone because they ask our forgiveness. People can forgive others from a position of strength when they feel confident that the violence and abuse they received are no longer threats to them. No one can offer forgiveness while holding on to the victim mentality. God, as the example of forgiveness, offered to forgive us from a position of strength. He was free to offer forgiveness to the world because we do not have any power over him. When Pontius Pilate said to Jesus, "Don't you know I have the power to save your life?" Jesus answer him, "You have no power over me unless it is given to you from above" (Jn. 19). God is above people's petty sins. Human behaviors and attitudes cannot damage him. He has the authority to offer forgiveness to those who rebelled against him on the account of Christ. God's forgiveness is an act of grace, and he is free to exercise his grace at any time he chooses. But even in God's case, men cannot experience God's forgiveness until after repentance and confession. That is, even God chooses not to force people to receive forgiveness. He can only make it available.

It goes without saying that we are not God. It is also clear that our ability to forgive from a position of strength is more limited than God's. But in order for us to be able to offer forgiveness to a perpetrator, we must be at peace with ourselves and with God. If we rush to offer forgiveness before we are ready, it could have negative consequences. Let me share two dangers people can experience when they offer forgiveness from a position of weakness.

First, it is very likely that an offer of forgiveness from a position of weakness will not be sincere or effective. Several issues could also come into play. People might have felt manipulated into forgiving a perpetrator before they were prepared to deal with the anxiety created by the injury or before they had resolved the contradiction. Additionally, injured people could be making the decision out of false guilt by believing that God expects them to patch things up sooner rather than later. Chances are they could have misunderstood God's requirement in this process. Another problem with a premature forgiveness is that we may have the wrong motives, i.e. we could offer forgiveness so that others can see how disgusting he is or to get pity. Many times, forgiveness could be motivated by false guilt. If people feel guilty as a result of a sermon that put into question their sincerity and their faith, some may act on an impulse before they are spiritually and emotionally ready to face the person responsible for the trauma.

Second, when people offer forgiveness from a position of weakness, they may end up feeling betrayed. This is especially true when they are not convinced the perpetrator has earned or deserves forgiveness. His unrepentant spirit will cause more damage than good. A premature act of forgiveness could reopen the spiritual wound and it could undo all the work done over the years. The injured person needs to forgive the perpetrator, but not as a means to restore the perpetrator to fellowship. If perpetrators want restoration to fellowship, they must deal with their own guilt and seek reconciliation through a process of confession and repentance. It is not up to the victims to restore perpetrators. This is the reason that forgiveness in this context is done for the benefit of the injured person. That is, when injured people extend forgiveness they eliminate the need for revenge, and with it, the anger and resentment that causes so much spiritual and emotional damage. If perpetrators confess and repent, that will be a collateral benefit to the forgiveness process. But restoration of the perpetrator is not the primary concern in this step. Additionally, perpetrators' restoration is not up to the victim. His restoration depends on his relationship with God and his ability to repent of his sins against the victim.

Let me add a couple more thoughts on the issue of forgiveness. Since forgiveness is an act of grace, no one is under any obligation to extend grace to everyone they know. God can extend unlimited grace because he is fully satisfied with himself and he has all the power in the universe to overcome (if he needed to do such a thing) any spiritual disappointment he might experience. He has eternal patience. He lives from eternity to eternity, and he is not concerned with wasting time by spending it on someone who has demonstrated a willingness to cause harm. And even God stated that his mercy (forgiveness) is a choice he makes. The Bible stated that, "I will have mercy on whom I will have mercy" (Ex. 33:19; Rom. 9:18). That is, while God is obligated to extend his grace to everyone indiscriminately, he has also established the parameters for people to seek and experience his grace and forgiveness. In God's economy, forgiveness becomes effective when people come to him in faith.

We, on the other hand, are limited creatures with limited resources and time. There is no way I want to spend my waking days seeking reconciliation with people who have victimized me when I can be friends with countless people who respect me. This is a key point because while the standard for us is to seek peace and live in peace with everyone, this is to be done as far as it depends on us (Rom. 12:18). That is, I will seek peace with everyone, but I cannot force anyone to be at peace with me.

As a matter of perspective, there are about seven billion people on this planet and on any given day I may know 250 of them. The other six billion do not feel abandoned by me, and I have no personal obligation to be friends with any of them. The question is, why create the impression that I cannot survive if I cannot become friends with a perpetrator? God is not requiring a phony guilt from us. The bottom line is that we need to heal if we are going to offer forgiveness from a position of strength. The point is that until we have mended our relationship with God and have accepted his design and purpose for us, we cannot be thinking of working with people who have injured and damaged us. As I conclude, I want to make a few final suggestions. Let me give you one hope and two goals.

Hope: Learning to Live with the Limp

The Bible related the story of Jacob (Gen. 32:22-32). Jacob wanted more than anything in his life to be in fellowship with God. He craved God's favor and blessing. We recognize that Jacob was more ambitious that was healthy for him, but he truly wanted God's favor in his life. He was willing to do almost anything to get it, as was evident by his deception to obtain his father's blessing.

Jacob cheated his brother out of his father's blessing, and he spent most of his life deceiving and running. As most of us know, "what goes around comes around," and Jacob had to return to his homeland and come face to face with his brother Esau. Jacob took all the necessary steps to reconcile with his brother. Something astounding happened on his way back – God met Jacob on the way in a place called Bethel. There, Jacob wrestled with the Angel of the Lord all night (initially identified as a man). The biblical passage portrays the event as if Jacob was involved in hand-to-hand combat with God. Almost at daybreak, the Angel of the Lord touched Jacob on his hip, leaving an injury for Jacob as a reminder that he had fought with the Lord and had overcome.

The injury caused a permanent limp in Jacob. But another remarkable thing happened to him there. His name was changed from Jacob to Israel to erase the deceitful past and to begin a new life as a prince of God. He would no longer be remembered as the one who lied to his father about his name. On this occasion, when the Angel of the Lord asked him for his name, Jacob finally came to terms with what his name implied for him. In those days, people's names were symbolic of their characters. Jacob was now ready to move in a different direction. Not only was his name changed to erase his tawdry past, but he was given a limp as a sign that his encounter with God had changed his life.

Before Jacob (Ja'aqob) the man crossed into the land of the blessing (jabboq), he had to wrestle (ye'abeq) with God. The play on words is significant. Matthews stated that, "The passage heightens the name "Jacob," for it conveyed as much as anything the selfish character he exhibited until his transformation at the Jabbok."[28] The event became symbolic so that people could find peace and recognize that perfection was not a requirement to be in an intimate relationship with God. The fact that the match lasted until daybreak is also significant. The darkness symbolized Jacob's situation at that

---

[28]   Mathews, K. A. (2005). *Genesis 11:27–50:26* (Vol. 1B, p. 556). Nashville: Broadman & Holman Publishers.

time. If he had known that he was fighting God, he would not have engaged him. He had to live differently. Jacob the schemer became Israel, a prince of God. He accepted his limp not as a curse, but as a blessing. Even his perception of self-changed.

Like Jacob, we have to change how we see ourselves in relationship to God. God sees us as heirs to his Kingdom, and he wants us to get into the Land of Blessing. But we have to stop hiding our limp. Jacob, like us, always had a spiritual limp. He was always crippled by his scheming ways. God exposed his deceitfulness and made it visible, so he would never forget that God knew him all along. It finally dawned on Jacob that God cannot be deceived, but that he can be merciful even to a schemer like Jacob. We need to learn to live with the limp (the result of the handicap we have developed from our spiritual injuries and irreconcilable contradictions). These contradictions are not determinative in our relationship with God unless we hide from his presence and break fellowship with him. But in order to do so, we have to wrestle with the inner man that is broken, until God blesses us at daybreak when we can really see who we really are in the presence of God.

Two Goals

First, God desires that we serve him and have him as our highest priority in order to restore the proper perspective of our relationship with him. This is an act of worship. He is the Creator, and no one else can take his place. Our recognition and acceptance of God's supremacy over creation and over our lives is of primary importance. We were created to be in a loving relationship with him. This has to be our greatest pursuit in life. The first commandment is very emphatic: "You shall have no other gods before me" (Ex. 20:3). He is our peace and our salvation. He sent Jesus to reconcile us unto himself and all we need is to receive his provision.

Second, God wants us to have peace with ourselves, with others, and with him. In the same way that our relationship with God is reciprocal, so it is with our relationship with our neighbor. We need to make every effort to love our neighbor and to forgive their trespasses against us. But when the neighbor is unrepentant and does not want to receive us, we should "go into the streets and say, 'Even the dust of your town that sticks to our feet we wipe off against you' . . ." (Lk. 10:10-11). Forgive me for taking some interpretational indulgence. Jesus freed the disciples from any responsibility for the lives of those who rejected them. A consistent interpretation would also free us from seeking friendship with perpetrators who have violated our dignity, damaged our intimacy mechanism and, literally, turned us into God's enemies.

We were not created to be victims or victimizers. We were created to be free. We were created to rule with God as his stewards here on earth. It is time to return back to God and to repair all the damage that we have caused each other.

APPENDIX A

List of Spiritual Injuries

1. Physical, Psychological, or Sexual abuse
2. Verbal Abuse
3. Religious Disappointment (God does not love me, there is too much evil and suffering in the world)
4. Abandonment by: family, friends, Spouse, God
5. Parents' divorce
6. Personal divorce
7. Loss: death, separation from parents, separation from children
8. Academic failures
9. Sports failures
10. Career failures (getting fired, not been able to perform at the job's expectation)
11. Demotions
12. Job transfers as a form of punishment
13. Betrayals by: family, friends, spouse, God
14. Low self-esteem: ("I am unlovable." "Other people don't like me." "I don't like myself." "I am unworthy." "I should not succeed.")
15. Shame for past behaviors
16. Shame for present behaviors
17. Shame of self (for who I have become – unable to finish task or to achieve personal or professional goals)
18. Anger directed to: family, friends, people in general, God
19. Unable to forgive: holding onto permanent grudges
20. Hatred: a desire to get even by inflicting pain on someone who hurt us
21. Personal disappointments ("I am not what I dream of being.")

22. Dissatisfied with job and/or profession
23. Embarrassment for present condition
24. Angry with self for getting to this point
25. Feelings of failure as a father/mother ("I did not/have not spend enough time with children.")
26. Feelings of failure as a husband/wife ("I should have stayed married." "I should have been a better husband/wife" "I don't know why I keep failing in my marriages.")
27. Feelings of failure as a son/daughter ("I should have treated my parent with more respect." "I should have realized sooner how much they loved me." "I should become closer to them.")
28. Discrimination: racial, sexual, cultural

ABOUT THE AUTHOR

Pastor Luis Scott graduated from Moody Bible Institute in 1986 with a Bachelor of Arts degree in Bible Theology with a Greek Emphasis. He received a Master of Divinity from Northern Baptist Theological Seminary in Lombard, Illinois in June of 1990. While serving the United States army as a chaplain, Pastor Scott completed the Clinical Pastoral Education at Eisenhower Medical Center. After 20 years of service Pastor Scott retired from the army in 2007.

Upon his retirement Pastor Scott accepted God's calling in June 2007 to plant Ambassadors of Christ Ministries in Columbus, GA. The ministry includes an English-speaking congregation (Ambassadors of Christ Fellowship), and a Spanish-speaking congregation (Iglesia Embajadores de Cristo). Additionally, Ambassadors of Christ Ministries established Life Skills University. LSU is one of the educational arms of the ministry developing leaders within the church and serving the community.

Pastor Scott is married to his high school sweetheart, Iris. They will celebrate their 39th anniversary together in 2018. They have four grown children, three daughters-in-law, one son-in-law and eight grandchildren.

CPSIA information can be obtained
at www.ICGtesting.com
Printed in the USA
LVHW111535031122
732318LV00018B/178

9 781949 804584